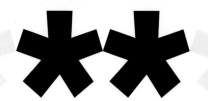

acknowledgements

This book is written and compiled by people who organise events, those who are suppliers to the events industry plus other experts in various related fields and grateful thanks are due to them for their contributions.

It is designed to offer practical help and guidance for organisers by providing advice, information and checklists and we also advise you to refer to the Guide to Health, Safety and Welfare at Music and Similar Events.

The authors would particularly like to thank the following for their expert contributions:

Automobile Association
Signage

AVT Ltd
Audio visuals and stage set

Boldscan Banners & Frames
Banners

CCH Editions Ltd
VAT on sponsorship and donations

Complete Talent Agency
Contracts with agents

Eve Trakway
Barriers; fencing; temporary access bridges; pedestrian walkways and coverings; temporary access roads; temporary access bridges

Mike Fulford
Consultant, Leisure Advice
Public consultation; procurement; catering

Robin Ireland
Healthstart
Fun run checklist

David James
Director, Arena Marketing
Marketing; promotion

Kalamazoo Security Print Ltd
Ticketing

Richard Limb
Director, Symonds Group
Event safety management; health and safety management; venue site and design

Made-up Textiles Association (MUTA)
Marquees and tents

Penny Mellor
Event Management Consultant
Welfare services

Mobile and Outside Caterers Association (GB) Ltd (MOCA)
Catering

Pains Fireworks
Fireworks

Barrie Smale
Smale Consulting
Time Management Matrix

Brian Strange
Director of Finance,
ILAM Services
Financial management

Anthony Tidy
Marketing Co-ordinator, Identilam plc
Badges and passes

Steve Warner
Weather Direct
Insurance

Zap Productions
Street entertainment

Contributions from the authors

All aspects of event management not attributed to specific experts were written by the authors, Sue Stayte and David Watt

events:
from **start** to **finish**

second edition

Co authors:
Sue Stayte and David C Watt

+

contributions from other industry experts

ILAM
Institute of Leisure and Amenity Management

Institute of Leisure and Amenity Management
ILAM House, Lower Basildon, Reading RG8 9NE
Tel: 01491 874800   Fax: 01491 874801
e-mail: info@ilam.co.uk
web: www.ilam.co.uk

ISBN 0 9542190 3 1

contents

c) crisis management

Points to consider when planning for a crisis:

- when planning an event, anticipate the worst possible scenario and make preparations accordingly
- devise a detailed crisis management plan and identify responsibilities within it
- be prepared to demonstrate human concern for what has happened
- whenever possible look for ways of using the media as part of your armoury for containing the effects of the crisis
- establish a 'war room' or emergency control centre and staff it with senior personnel trained to fulfil specific roles designed to contain and manage the crisis
- know your event and listen to staff on the ground
- avoid the use of jargon. Use language that shows you care about what has happened and which clearly demonstrates that you are trying to put matters right
- know your audience/customers and their requirements
- whenever possible, seek outside expert advice when drawing up crisis contingency plans. Don't reinvent the wheel
- training for all staff is an integral part of planning to deal with crisis

d) event business and budget planning process

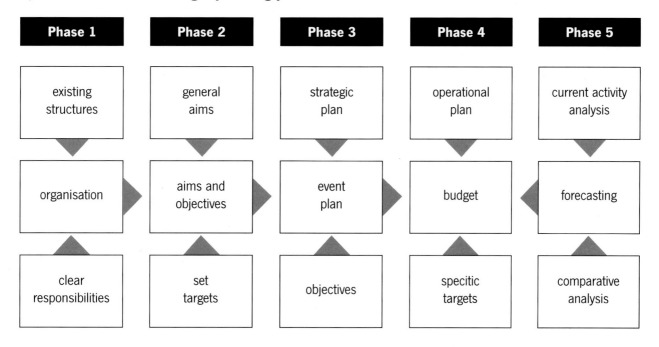

Phase 1	Phase 2	Phase 3	Phase 4	Phase 5
existing structures	general aims	strategic plan	operational plan	current activity analysis
organisation	aims and objectives	event plan	budget	forecasting
clear responsibilities	set targets	objectives	specific targets	comparative analysis

e) critical path

TASK	Year in advance	9 months	6 months	3 months	1 month	1 week
eg Compile budget						
eg Identify personnel						
eg Book venue						
eg First team meeting						

introduction

This book is a revision of the original Events from Start to Finish publication written in 1997. We have added sections on financial management, procurement, specifications, health and safety, venue and site design; temporary access roads and bridges, installing pedestrian walkways as well as additional checklists.

This publication has been produced to enable people working in all aspects of the events industry to have access to some practical advice and support documentation to make their working life a little easier.

It is unashamedly practical and made up of lists, examples and advice drawn from a variety of sources and put together through various individuals' and organisations' experience over many years. It supplies a variety of practical tools to individuals and groups setting out to organise an event for whatever purpose. The organiser is merely left with the decision as to which of these tools are of particular use to them for any particular event.

It is also hoped that organisers will draw upon these materials as a reference for training courses they attend, or indeed for training courses they put together internally for a group of involved people – either on a paid or voluntary basis

Materials from this book have been drawn together from a variety of sources – groups and individuals working in the industry and that has allowed a comprehensive package to be put together. It is hoped that people involved in the business will continue to seek help and advice from each other, as one of the key areas for information must be colleagues practising in the business. The development for partnerships and support networks is going to be an essential part of improving event provision and the ability to learn from others in the field is a key skill.

chapter one

events

a) what are they?

Defining events is always difficult – they can be many and varied and require a whole range of different skills.

Fundamentally, an event is something out of the ordinary, which has to be specially provided for. It can range from a monthly committee meeting to an international tournament, from a village fete to a major multicultural festival and from the local dramatic society performance to a high-profile film premier.

Venues, audiences, funding arrangements and the organisational structures and methods can all be radically different in specific instances, but

No matter how large or small the event, it is vitally important that each one is considered separately and that each event is appropriately considered and efficiently organised.

b) aims and objectives

Every event must have a clearly stated aim, otherwise the event probably should not happen.

Events demand a lot of concentrated effort and commitment. This commitment can only come out of a genuine belief, among all the participants, that they are worthwhile and that they will be beneficial.

As well as an overall purpose, any specific event must have its own set of objectives, which must be clear and be set down in a way which will allow the organiser to judge the success of their event after completion.

Objectives must be:

- specific
- measurable
- agreed
- understood
- clear
- achievable
- realistic
- simple
- unambiguous
- timed
- appropriate
- relevant

In short, it is essential that event objectives should always be:

S M A R T

Specific — to the particular event and particular aspects of it

Measurable — express the objective in numbers and quantities

Agreed — make sure all team members know the objectives

Realistic — set objectives that the team can realistically achieve

Timed — set a timescale for achievement of the objectives

> "Oh, let us never, never doubt what nobody is sure about"
>
> *Hilaire Belloc*
> *1870-1953*

chapter two
feasibility

a) where to start?

Carrying out a feasibility study is a fundamental part of the event planning process. You will need to gather all the information required to provide you with a clear picture of the possibility of success for your event.

There are various methods of research which can be undertaken:

- an evaluation of last year's event (attendance figures, databases, customer feedback, etc)
- questionnaire surveys
- telephone surveys
- face to face interviews
- other organisations' events and how they work
- use of the internet/other technology
- government agencies
- professional bodies
- trade associations and directories
- newspapers
- television/radio
- articles in the trade press
- public consultation

Check that you are not breaching the Data Protection Act if you are storing and using personal data on customers, participants, attendants, etc and make sure that your evidence is valid and reliable.

In reporting your investigations to the decision-makers, you will need to have made sound judgments about the type, quality and quantity of information to be presented to ensure you provide a balanced view. The aim of your report should be to present factual information and should provide a summary and recommendations. It will probably be this report on which is based the decision to stage, or not to stage, the event.

The items listed in your report are probably basic questions and all of these (and more, depending on the type of event) should be answered before you commence work on any of the detailed planning.

b) so what do I do now?

Having answered these questions you should now be much clearer about what you are doing and how and why you are doing it. You should have quite a clear and positive picture and be ready to proceed confidently.

However, if this is not the case and you are organising the event because somebody has told you to, or you are still unclear about some of the answers to these questions, don't despair. It is quite normal for organisers to have some gaps in their ideas when they first sit down to plan an event. Probably the best course of action is to refer to the end of this book and seek more help. Don't be embarrassed about learning from other people's expertise. It is always better than learning from your own mistakes.

A structured programme of public consultation is fundamental to the organisation and development of a programme of events.

c) public consultation

Public consultation will:

- identify the aspirations of the community
- identify the priorities of the community
- identify the input that the community wishes to make
- build on the expertise available in the community
- provide an opportunity to share information

It is essential that the consultation takes place within a strategic framework and within set financial parameters. Unless this is done, public ideas and expectations may rise to a level that is beyond that which can be provided by the organiser. Consultation must also take place early in the decision making process.

A key component of consultation should be with local organisations, schools, trade organisations, community associations and organisations consulted on previous events. Wherever possible, this consultation ought to be on a 'face to face' basis.

Consideration may also be given to involving representatives of the community on a steering group. However, such organisations are likely to have vested interests and will, therefore, be in a difficult position when it comes to taking an overview. One of the roles of any steering group will be to endorse that a programme of public consultation is undertaken.

Mike Fulford, Consultant with Leisure Advice, supplied this section on public consultation and his details can be found in the back of this book.

d) example questions for a feasibility study

Question	Answer
Why do you need to stage this event?	
What is the title/theme of the event?	
Is the event celebrating a particular anniversary/should it be branded to reflect the anniversary?	
When will it be held? Is the timing right?	
Will it be school holiday time? If so, how will this affect attendance?	
Where will it be held?	
Are there detailed event objectives?	
What costs are involved?	
From where are the potential income sources derived?	
Who will organise it?	
Who will attend?	
Who attended the previous event?	
Does the proposed site have suitable access for disabled and elderly people?	
Have you considered all the local bye-laws which may have an effect on the event?	
Do you have sufficient support staff?	
Have you allowed sufficient planning time?	
Who will prepare a contingency plan? (e.g. How will inclement weather conditions affect the event?)	
How will it be publicised?	
Is it attractive to a sponsor?	
Are there any competing events?	
Is the programme content topical?	
Is there a fee or is it free entry? (Licensing application may affect your decision as to whether to charge an entry fee or not)	
Is the event likely to cause nuisance to nearby residents?	

chapter three
planning

Events are important to the participants, the organisers and the activity and they need a professional and thorough approach to their planning.

Earlier we gave a somewhat simplistic view of events when defining them as something that happens. This may suggest that they happen by themselves – nothing could be further from the truth. People will be required to make them happen.

Also, the crucial difference between what you might call 'routine' events and 'special' events are that special events must always be planned or they will not be 'special'.

Planning will fall into a variety of stages, but it must be stressed that, regardless of the size of event, each of these stages must be gone through. Obviously, depending on the size of the event, the length of each planning stage will vary.

a) event planning stages

- determine aims and objectives
- formulate policy
- carry out a feasibility study
- make decision to go ahead (or not)
- compile budget
- identify personnel
- identify resources
- identify event requirements
- identify tasks
- define structure
- communicate structure
- create detailed plan and timescale
- establish control systems
- plan event – presentation, preparation, implementation and recovery
- finalise accounts
- hold debriefing
- compile and circulate final evaluation report

REMEMBER

Proper
Planning
Promotes
Perfect
Performance

OR

Proper
Planning
Prevents
Pathetic
Performance

You will have to identify the resources required:

- physical
- professional
- financial

All events should be F A M O U S

Feasible	it should be possible for the team concerned to achieve the aims
Appropriate	the organisers and participants should be suited to the task
Meaningful	the event should have value to customers (and to team members)
Organised	aims should be well thought-out and clearly stated
United	there should be a shared understanding of the aims, matched by the commitment to achieve them
Supported	adequate resources should be identified

REMEMBER WHEN PLANNING YOUR PROJECT, SUCCESSFUL EVENTS NEED...

- appropriate implementation mechanisms
- budgeting
- business plan/feasibility study
- clear objectives
- committed personnel
- contingency plans
- creativity and innovation
- customer care
- detailed programming
- emergency procedures
- entertainment
- evaluation and control (formative & summative)
- financial control
- flexibility
- good management and strong leadership
- hard work and enthusiasm
- leadership and co-ordination
- logistical planning
- marketing (especially promotion)
- measurable targets
- media interest
- participants
- planning and documentation
- post-event evaluation
- pricing policy
- public consultation
- quality not quantity
- resources and facilities
- risk assessment
- structure and good communications
- support (from public, volunteers, politicians, etc)
- teamwork and good interpersonal relationships
- time
- sense of humour

b) organisational plan

An event, like any business venture, needs a clear plan in the background; a clear context in which to deliver and monitor its purpose.

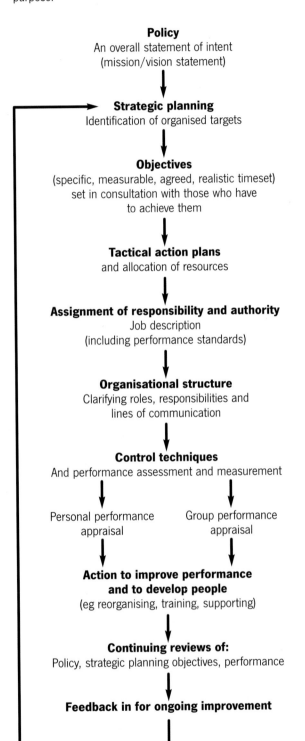

Policy
An overall statement of intent
(mission/vision statement)

Strategic planning
Identification of organised targets

Objectives
(specific, measurable, agreed, realistic timeset)
set in consultation with those who have
to achieve them

Tactical action plans
and allocation of resources

Assignment of responsibility and authority
Job description
(including performance standards)

Organisational structure
Clarifying roles, responsibilities and
lines of communication

Control techniques
And performance assessment and measurement

Personal performance appraisal

Group performance appraisal

**Action to improve performance
and to develop people**
(eg reorganising, training, supporting)

Continuing reviews of:
Policy, strategic planning objectives, performance

Feedback in for ongoing improvement

f) event planning chart

Taken from: Leisure and Tourism for Intermediate GNVQ by Outhart et al

---

OUTLINE THE OBJECTIVES

remember SMART and FAMOUS

DESCRIBE THE EVENT

customers; timings; activities; movements

CALCULATE RESOURCES

finance; equipment; time; information; people; materials

IDENTIFY CONSTRAINTS

staff; opening times; facility capacity; transport; equipment; health; safety; security

---

CONTINGENCY ACTIONS

emergencies; disruptions; changes

ALLOCATE ROLES

function; team structures; communication/reporting

---

g) event planning requirements

Having identified the overall planning progressions, it is necessary to be more specific and identify the precise process by detailing all the requirements for the event. This can be a time-consuming procedure, but should involve a number of people who can think in the widest possible way in an attempt to try and identify all the possible items which will be required to deliver a successful event.

Such a list, which can never really be all encompassing, is necessary to allow detailed planning and implementation to go ahead (see the Master Checklist later in the book). The aim here is to identify every single heading that needs to be covered and under each heading, every single item that will be required to produce an efficient, effective event of a quality appropriate to the level of the event.

This means going through a very precise thought process, no matter how large or small, endeavouring to ensure that nothing which is required is omitted.

h) event organiser's checklist

☐ specify the nature of the event

☐ define event objectives

☐ select a delivery strategy

☐ develop a list of specific requirements

☐ work out a schedule

☐ produce a detailed budget

☐ identify the event team

☐ decide on roles and responsibilities

☐ devise organisational structure

☐ specify operational plan

☐ write operations manual

☐ train team members

☐ deliver outcomes

☐ monitor progress

☐ take corrective action

☐ provide feedback

☐ dispose of surplus equipment, materials and supplies

☐ evaluate event performance

☐ carry out event debrief

☐ complete final audit

☐ complete event report

i) Gantt chart

A Gantt chart is a horizontal bar chart which graphically displays the time relationship of the stages in an event. It is named after Henry Gantt, the industrial engineer who introduced the chart in the early 1900s. Each stage of the event is represented by a line placed on the chart in the time period when it is to be undertaken. Once complete the Gantt chart shows the flow of activities in sequence as well as those that can be under way at the same time.

To create a Gantt chart, list the stages required to achieve an event and estimate the time required for each. Then list the stages down the left side of the chart and time intervals along the bottom. Draw a line across the chart for each stage, starting at the planned beginning date and ending on the completion date.

Some parallel steps can be carried out at the same time with one taking longer than the other. This allows some flexibility about when to start the shorter stage as long as the plan has it finished in time to flow into subsequent stages. This situation can be shown with a dotted line continuing onto the line when the step must be completed.

When your Gantt chart is finished, you will be able to see the minimum total time for the project, the proper sequence of stages and which stages can be under way at the same time.

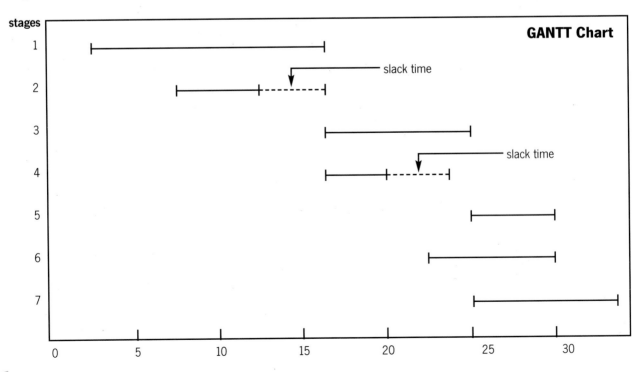

chapter four

personal management

People involved in events will require a number of personal management skills.

These personal management skills will be required at a variety of levels depending on the degree of involvement and authority that the individual has and the scale of the event. However, no matter what the individual's involvement in events, improved personal management skills will help increase the effectiveness of their input.

In essence, personal management leads to increased personal effectiveness, which in turn leads to increased organisational effectiveness and event delivery.

It is absolutely essential that individuals are able to organise themselves and prioritise their workload to lead to maximum efficiency in their own personal organisation: it seems unlikely that anyone who cannot organise themselves will be able to organise an event.

a) time management

Time management is a key area of personal management which is often not practised well, even by people who can manage quite effectively in other ways. Busy people, as events organisers tend to be, always want more time in the day and since there are only a finite number of hours, minutes and seconds in any one day, the only way to find them is to get the maximum use out of each minute that passes.

Time management can involve some fairly complicated procedures and this book is not the place to consider them all. However, there are some principles worth mentioning.

- It is always beneficial to start by analysing your normal time used to see if there are any aspects of your programme which can be altered - particularly if there are any time-wasters in terms of structures, systems or people, that can be minimised within your personal operation

- An over-abundance of paper is a very common example of something that could be dramatically reduced to give someone more time for constructive work

- It is helpful to organise all emails and telephone calls, and

indeed any tasks to be undertaken, by grading them one to five, and doing the ones which are the most important first of all

- It is also common for many people to just achieve the easy tasks and leave the more difficult ones on the back burner all the time. Achieving big tasks does create more time and also makes the individual feel-good factor rise.

Complete the matrix below and think carefully (and be honest) about the way you spend time currently. Think carefully and be realistic about the targets you are going to set. Once you have undertaken this part of the exercise, draft an action plan template, reflect on it, discuss it with others, fine tune it and then **DO IT**.

	Urgent	**Not Urgent**
IMPORTANT	**1** % time you spend here = Target % time to spend here in future =	**2** % time you spend here = Target % time to spend here in future =
NOT IMPORTANT	**3** % time you spend here = Target % time to spend here in future =	**4** % time you spend here = Target % time to spend here in future =

This matrix is taken from a Managers' Training Workshop delivered by Barrie Smale of Smale Consulting Ltd – details of this organisation can be found at the back of the book.

b) meetings

In so many event settings there seems to be so much time spent (often wasted) in meetings. If you are going to plan an event then meetings will be necessary, but certain simple principles will remove excessive meetings and ensure that those we must have are held efficiently and effectively.

In terms of managing meetings we have to:

* minimise the number of meetings
* ensure those that we do have are as short as possible
* have an agenda, a time limit for the overall meeting and a time limit for each agenda item
* each individual should prepare for each meeting
* have your own individual objectives as well as those for the overall meeting
* every meeting should have minutes or notes taken
* a timed action plan should result from each meeting – if this is not the case then why did everyone attend in the first place?

c) leadership

If you are going to manage, organise or lead an event you will have to portray some significant leadership skills:

positive qualities	negative qualities
organised	self-centred
always gets results	moody
patient	gossip
approachable	dictatorial
decisive	intimidatory
interested	doesn't understand
enthusiastic	condescending
assertive	poor attention to detail
communicative	uncommunicative
listens and acts	shy and nervous
firm but fair	fixed views
punctual	unappreciative
confident	
good motivator	

d) the team

You might want your team members to have the following qualities, skills, abilities and characteristics:

enthusiastic	flexible	available
courteous	responsible	good communicator
sense of humour	organised	willing
energetic	initiative	reliable
trustworthy	dependable	unflappable
friendly	teamworker	honest
punctual	efficient	personable
knowledgeable	committed	interested
pro-active	articulate	diligent
resourceful	ability to cope under pressure	

As a leader, you will be responsible for people's performance. Utilise the following management actions as necessary to your specific event to ensure you get the best from your team, whether they are paid staff or volunteers:

consult	inform	appraise
inspire	lead	listen
control	delegate	recruit
make decisions	understand	guide
co-ordinate	monitor	liaise
care	communicate	encourage
evaluate	schedule	supervise
direct	anticipate	discuss
analyse	brainstorm	question
solve problems	review	set goals

> "Take care of the pence and the pounds will take care of themselves"
> *William Lowndes 1652–1724*

chapter five

financial planning

This chapter considers the financial planning issues to consider when organising events.

While it may appear to be unnecessary to have a separate business plan for a simple event, it should be treated like any other business venture. Going through the process of determining the aims and objectives of the event, financial or otherwise, can help the organiser focus on the key areas which will enable the aims and objectives to be achieved.

Is there a financial objective for the event? It may not be necessary for the event to achieve a surplus if the organisation is prepared to subsidise it. There may be a specific financial target. However, whatever this is it needs to be clear at the outset as this will clearly impact on the plans for the event, in particular the budget.

Events must have clear, precise and accurate budgeting. Before preparing a budget it is important for the organiser to understand the nature of both the costs involved and the income received, as well as other financial issues such as VAT, inflation, insurance and foreign exchange.

The organiser must also consider how financial risks can be addressed, as well as the impact on cash flow and cash handling.

a) income

i) ticket pricing

There are any number of factors which may determine how much can be charged for an event. In determining the price to be charged for tickets, consideration must be given to:

- whether VAT should be charged (See VAT Implications page 19)
- whether there be a concessionary price, e.g. for students or families
- if the event is to be held over several days, whether the event can be sold on the basis of half-day, whole-day or whole-event tickets.
- whether external funding will enable or require

admission to be free or subsidised (See below)
- what competitors charge for similar events

ii) other income

The potential to generate income from an event is not limited to admission; other potential sources of income could include merchandising, catering concessions, grant-aid and sponsorship.

iii) external funding

For many events, finding external funding is the crucial issue and is the one which requires most work, especially if there is the possibility that the costs of running the event may not be covered from admission prices.

Given the correct event, the correct aim, with the correct objectives then additional external funding can be found. It must be presented as a package to the potential funder in order to have a chance of funding being obtained successfully.

There are many agencies that can have a significant interest in supporting events to ensure they happen successfully in a given location. The more obvious ones are local authorities and local tourist boards but there are others, for example:

- hoteliers
- local chambers of commerce
- national agencies, e.g. arts councils or sports councils
- major local employers
- national lottery distributing bodies

Grant-aiding bodies will work within a timeframe whereby grants are approved in advance for any particular financial year, giving the organisers financial certainty that their events will be supported.

b) costs

The event organiser needs to understand the nature of costs. Only then can an event budget be prepared. The following considers different types of costs as they relate to a specific event (rather than to the whole organisation) as while a cost may be fixed in terms of an event, it would be a cost that would vary according to the number of events that were organised.

i) fixed costs

Fixed costs apply to those items that do not directly change according to the level of activity. Fixed costs could include:

- hire of the venue (unless the contract linked the fee to ticket sales)
- costs of producing the event programme and promoting the event. (While the majority of the cost will be incurred prior to the event, it may be necessary to reprint an amended programme and incur extra distribution costs in order to attract additional participants)
- insurance costs (again be aware that the cost may be banded according to the turnover of the event)

ii) semi-fixed costs

Certain costs although essentially 'fixed', may well vary, for example, if the ticket sales exceed certain numbers. Such costs would include:

- hiring more space at the venue.
- employing additional staff
- additional insurance cover.

iii) variable costs

These are the costs that would change according to the level of activity or the number of participants. Variable costs could include:

- catering, such as providing lunches if included with the ticket price, and if charged on a per head basis. However, the unit cost may change according to the numbers, and could be higher if numbers fall below original estimates.
- the costs of communicating with each participant, for example, sending booking confirmations, maps etc.

iv) semi-variable costs

Certain costs may only be variable incrementally, due, for example, to minimum or fixed order quantities. These may include any items given to the participants that may have to be purchased in units of 50 or 100.

v) marginal cost

It is important to be aware of the marginal cost of each additional person attending the event. In many circumstances the marginal cost would be the same as the variable cost (see above) as it would usually represent the direct extra cost of each additional person attending. Any income received above the marginal cost will be a contribution to profit. Knowing the marginal cost will enable the organiser to determine, for example, the minimum price for concessions or how much discount can be given to group bookings.

vi) sunk costs

These costs tend to be up-front costs which, once incurred, cannot be recovered whether the event proceeds or is cancelled. Such cost could include:

- the staff time spent in preparation, including the costs of visiting potential venues.
- advance promotional material
- any non-refundable deposits on venues

vii) indirect costs

All of the above costs could be considered to be direct costs. However, there are certain costs that may be incurred but may not be charged directly to the event, as other departments will absorb them. These may include:

- accounting costs, including bank charges, and those related to processing sales and purchase invoices.
- any input from other departments, such as the staff input into designing promotional material (if done in-house), the costs of legal advice on contracts etc.

The organiser needs to be aware of the potential of incurring such costs and the potential impact on the event. It may be necessary to check that there will be sufficient resources available in order that the organisation is able to contribute to the staging of the event.

viii) accounting for staff costs

Given that event organisation is a service, in common with the provision of many other services, labour costs are a significant element of the cost base. Whether and how staff costs are being charged directly to an event or not may depend on:

- whether additional agency or casual staff are employed. In this case it would be appropriate to charge such costs directly to the event.
- whether the event is one of many organised in-house by the organisation. In which case to allocate relevant staff costs to each event would require a suitable time-recording system.
- the extent to which direct and indirect staff overheads are included. While it would always be appropriate to include pension and other such costs there may be other indirect staff-related overheads, such as the costs of the human resources and accounts staff, which would be included dependent on the overhead allocation methodology used by the organisation.

c) other financial issues

i) VAT implications

Value Added Tax (VAT) and the effect it has on both income and expenditure must be taken into account.

The VAT status of the event may be determined by:

- whether the organiser is VAT registered
- the type of organisation (e.g. charity, local authority, limited company).
- the nature of the event (e.g. seminar, social, fundraising).
- the frequency of the event (e.g. one-off events may be treated differently for VAT purposes to recurring events).

The VAT status of the event must be determined very early in the planning process as this will, for example, impact on:

- whether the tickets prices are inclusive or exclusive of VAT.
- whether VAT incurred on expenditure will be recoverable or irrecoverable.
- the VAT status of different types of income may also vary. For example, the VAT status of sponsorship will be dependent on whether the sponsor receives any goods or services in return for their contribution, or whether it is purely a donation (See Chapter 11 (g)).
- it is important that the VAT position is clear on any booking forms, with the amount inclusive of VAT always clearly shown. This is important so that those attendees who are unable to recover VAT are aware of the total cost to them.

ii) inflation

Inflation can have quite profound consequences for budgeting. Estimates should be calculated on current figures but an awareness of the possible effects of inflation must be borne in mind. Calculations should be made and attached to the estimates, indicating what may happen to the funding of the event given likely inflationary trends. Agreeing contracts and fixing prices as far as possible in advance with suppliers can reduce the potential impact of inflation, although it may mean that it reduces choices available to the organiser, particularly if other more competitive suppliers are subsequently found.

iii) insurance

Insurance advice is given later in this book (see Chapter 9 [h]). Public liability and even perhaps limited personal accident insurance must be arranged, another item all too easily forgotten with potentially very expensive consequences.

iv) exchange rates/overseas income

If the event is to attract participants from outside the UK then foreign currency transactions may have an impact on finances.

- provide ticket prices in other relevant currencies, such as the euro. However, include within the foreign currency price a margin to absorb fluctuations in exchange rates or bank commission charges.
- consider whether the organisation has the accounting systems and resources to handle foreign currency transactions. Will foreign currency bank accounts be required?
- how should VAT be accounted for? If the organiser is VAT registered and the event income is standard rated then VAT will have to be charged on all ticket sales. However overseas participants may be able to recover the VAT they have paid from Customs & Excise.

If the event is to be very dependent on overseas visitors then not only will financial issues such as exchange rate fluctuations have an impact on attendance, but also non-financial matters should be considered such as fear of terrorism or disease, which will also increase the risks associated with the event.

d) preparing the budget

Having considered all of these issues, the organiser should now be able to prepare a budget for the event, having fully understood the issues relating to income, expenditure and VAT The latter is particularly important as when preparing a budget you must show income net of VAT and expenditure net of recoverable VAT.

i) budget assumptions

In preparing a budget a number of assumptions must be made. These would include:

- the number of people who would attend
- the price of tickets, which may include concessionary tickets.
- an estimate of the numbers purchasing each type of ticket
- other sources of income
- the activities occurring at the event (see below)
- the related direct costs, such as the venue, performers etc.
- the staffing required
- any other costs

Initially many of these may be purely estimated. It is important to try and estimate these costs as accurately as possible; under-estimated costs can be misleading and cause severe problems later in achieving the required financial out-turn, while over-estimated costs can make an otherwise profitable event appear not to be viable. However, it should be possible to accurately cost certain items as quotations are received and activities are finalised.

ii) assessing the financial impact of activities

The content of an event will drive all other factors. For each activity that is proposed to be included in the event it is important to determine:

- the benefit to the event from each activity (including the potential impact on ticket price and sales)

- any additional income that can be generated from the activity (e.g. from concessions, merchandising etc.)

- the estimated cost of each activity and how it can be monitored

- any financial risks associated with the activity (such as what if event merchandise does not sell?)

- the priority of the activity within the event as a whole (is it a peripheral activity or core to the success of the event?)

By considering all activities in this way, should it be necessary to reduce costs or change the content of the event for other reasons, the financial impact on the event can be readily identified.

iii) contingencies

It is always prudent to include in budget estimates for additional unforeseen items of cost. Depending on the size of the project in hand, it is advisable to allow between five and ten per cent of the total expenditure as an add-in for contingencies.

iv) finalising the budget

A first draft of the budget can be prepared once all the activities to be included in the event have been identified and all related income and expenditure has been estimated. If after determining all the content of the event the budget demonstrates that the financial target is being achieved then this can be taken forward as the initial budget. However, if this is not the case, the event will be need to be re-evaluated to decide where costs can be saved, without compromising on the quality or the safety of the event. Prudent budgeting must be recommended, as long as it is not unrealistically gloomy. However, it is always best to be cautious about income estimates and pessimistic about expenditure.

v) monitoring the budget

Review your budget regularly. A weekly monitoring system is recommended. Constantly revise and monitor your budget; don't be caught by unexpected cost trends. An example is given at the end of this chapter as to how the event budget may be revised as the trend in ticket sales becomes apparent, fixed costs are confirmed, and variable costs recalculated.

e) cash flow forecasting

A key element of financial planning is to understand when costs will be incurred and when income will be received. Dependent on the financial resources of the organisation, it may be necessary to finance the period between costs being incurred and income being received. Should it be likely that any significant additional financing costs may be incurred then these should be included in the budget, although possibly only as a memorandum item if it is likely to be absorbed elsewhere in the organisation.

Particular issues with the phasing of income and expenditure would include:

- having to pay a deposit on booking a venue. For a major event this can sometimes be several years in advance in order to guarantee availability.

- will tickets be prepaid or will it be necessary to invoice after the event? (In the latter case this could mean no income is received for at least 30 days.)

- what are the payment terms for the suppliers? Some may require 50% of the fee in advance; others may require payment within 7 days.

A cash flow forecast may be completed such as in the example at the end of this chapter. When, how much, and for how long expenditure exceeds income, and what cash balances are available, will determine whether any additional financing is necessary.

f) cash

No section on finance would be complete without considering cash. While the majority of transactions may well be cash-free, with the majority of income and expenditure transactions in cheques, credit cards etc, there may well be a requirement for some cash transactions.

i) petty cash

The only cash at an event may well be a small petty cash float, primarily for ad hoc expenses such as car parks, taxis and refreshments. It would still be advisable to:

- keep the cash in a lockable cash box

- make one member of staff responsible for it (with the key!)

- issue clear instructions on what petty cash is to be used for

- ensure a petty cash voucher is completed for each

transaction, with receipts provided whenever possible

- ensure that any cash floats are signed for by the individual
- keep the cash box in a secure place, such as a hotel safe, overnight.

ii) cash receipts

If cash is to be taken on admission then it may be necessary to consider how that cash is to be stored securely or safely removed from the site. It is likely that it will not be possible, due to bank opening times, to pay the cash directly into the bank on the day of the event. It may be necessary to arrange for a bank night safe facility to be available. It is advisable to make such arrangements well in advance to ensure that such a facility is available at a nearby branch and that there is sufficient time to obtain a night safe key.

When handling large quantities of cash it is essential that certain protocols are followed, including:

- always make sure two members of staff are involved in counting cash. This not only enables the cash counted to be double-checked, but also protects the individuals from being exposed to accusations of theft in the event of an apparent shortfall.
- where possible reconcile tickets sold to cash received.
- it is advisable when taking large quantities of cash to the bank for staff not to go alone for the sake of their own security.
- consider employing a security company to remove large amounts of cash.

It is also important to know what insurance cover there is in place to cover the theft of cash and to be aware of any conditions stipulated by the insurers.

g) financial risk

While prudent budgeting can itself minimise the financial risks of events, it is important to be aware of any potential financial risks. The organiser should attempt to identify those risks and then consider how that risk can be mitigated or reduced. Ultimately the organiser has to consider whether the organisation can afford to take the risk.

i) what are the potential financial risks?

The organiser needs to consider potential risks, which may include the following:

- what happens if the event has to be cancelled because of insufficient ticket sales? At what point should the decision to cancel be made?
- what are the cancellation clauses in the contract with the venue and other suppliers?

- will the costs of cancellation outweigh any potential financial loss from going ahead and running the event?
- what would be the wider impact on the organisation if the event were cancelled for purely financial reasons? Would cancellation cause the organisation to not meet particular objectives, which may, for example, impact on its external funding?
- what happens if headline performers do not turn up? Will participants ask to have their fees refunded?
- what are the sunk costs of the event if it is cancelled?
- what is the most you can lose if the event goes ahead?
- what is the risk of theft of cash or other items?

ii) reducing the financial risk

There are a number of ways to reduce the financial risk of organising an event. These include:

- finding an organisation to agree to underwrite any losses on the event.
- monitoring closely income and expenditure by regularly revising the budget.
- ensuring all ticket income is received prior to the event, reducing the risks of bad debts.
- allowing for the effects of inflation and exchange rate fluctuations in the budgeting process.
- ensuring there are financial controls in place to manage any cash received etc.
- ensuring there is adequate insurance cover in place.

This section on Financial Planning was provided by Brian Strange, Director of Finance at ILAM.

h) example of budget items

ITEM	Budget Forecast £	Revision 1 (Date) £	Revision 2 (Date) £	Revision 3 (Date) £	Revision 4 (Date) £
INCOME					
Ticket sales					
Sponsorship					
Donations					
Grants					
Concessions/franchises					
Stallholder income					
TOTAL INCOME					
EXPENDITURE					
Marketing					
Signage					
Artistes/performers					
Toilets					
Staging, lighting, sound					
Seating					
Licences					
Security					
Waste collection					
First aid					
Policing					
Insurance					
Barriers/fencing					
Marquees					
Photography					
Special effects (fireworks, lasers etc)					
Contingency (20% of total expenditure)					
TOTAL EXPENDITURE					

i) cash flow forecast

ITEM	MONTH												
	1	2	3	4	5	6	7	8	9	10	11	12
INCOME												
1												
2												
3												
Total												
EXPENDITURE												
1												
2												
3												
Total												
Opening Balance												
Surplus (deficit)												
Closing balance												

> "Necessity never made a good bargain"   *Benjamin Franklin 1706–90*

chapter six

procurement (purchasing)

Purchasing is a much under-rated activity – after all, we all go shopping!

As an everyday chore, our shopping choices are often guided by what is in the shop window display, catalogue, or on the supermarket shelf. For example, we may prepare a shopping list which includes tins of fruit, prior to visiting the supermarket, but we will use the shelf display to decide whether we want a large or small tin, whether the fruit is in juice or in syrup, which brand we would like, the price or the type of fruit.

Purchases on which we are to base our business success as event managers need a lot more preparation!

Just how much preparation will depend on a number of factors. These factors include:

a) value of the purchase

The more expensive the proposed purchase, the greater the likelihood of achieving a good return on the investment of time and money in a tendering process. The contract value might be calculated as a one off or as the total for a series of purchases over a period of time, made on one contract. Prospective suppliers will not want to be involved in expensive and time-consuming tendering processes for small-value contracts.

b) time

A tendering process takes time! Just how much time can vary but adequate provision must be made at the event planning stage. A sensible assessment needs to be made of both the time that you and your professional advisors require as well as the time that potential suppliers will need to provide a properly costed tender. Suppliers have holidays too, so make allowances if you want a good quality bid! The time required for the tender process is in addition to the lead-time that will be required once the written order has been made.

c) rules and regulations

These cannot be ignored and can come from a number of sources

Government – the public sector's purchasing is governed by national and international regulations which vary according to contract value and contract content.

Corporate – your own organisation may have its own internal standing orders and regulations governing purchasing. Whilst there is usually an exemption for low-value items, there is usually a requirement for competitive quotations for items above a certain value with the process becoming more complex and more regulated as the value increases.

Clients – If you are working as an event organiser on behalf of a client, such as a local authority or government funded organisation, then your contract with them will usually make their purchasing regulations binding upon you. Clearly you need to know what is required! Grant aided projects normally have to demonstrate accountability through transparency of the purchasing exercise. The financing of projects may be withheld where finance providers' regulations are not followed.

The market – The issue here is around the number of potential competitors for the work or product that you are going to put out to tender. It is difficult, but not impossible, to develop competitive tendering exercises for products and services that are either not currently available or for which there are few companies in the market place. Event organisers need to be aware of the dangers of combining a mix of products and services into one contract that does not match the profile of potential suppliers' businesses. The principle danger is either a lack of interest in bidding, or tender prices that have been marked up excessively and represent poor value for money.

Existing contracts – Always check that your organisation has not already established a 'nominated suppliers' list for particular categories of products or services requiring you to order from that supplier. Such a list will normally have been established by some sort of tendering process in the first instance. It will often provide some form of quantity discount for your organisation as a whole as well as a competitive unit price and doing away with the need for frequent tendering exercises.

Warning – whilst all sizeable organisations will have some regulations or standing orders governing purchasing, it should be noted that public authorities and charitable organisations will have extensive regulations. Not only will failure to adhere to these regulations be likely to be regarded as a serious disciplinary offence, but it may also constitute a criminal offence. Junior staff should ensure that they make themselves aware of an organisation's rules governing purchasing.

d) the stages in the purchasing process

Set out below are the stages in the purchasing process and an outline of the main features of each stage. Exactly which stages you need to follow and how much emphasis to put on each stage is a matter for you to decide according to circumstances.

- planning a purchase
- the specification
- price and payment clauses
- tender documents
- selecting and evaluating tenders
- awarding the contract
- monitoring the contract

e) planning a purchase

Work out the period of time required for seeking quotations or a formal tendering exercise, incorporating both practical and statutory requirements.

Make allowances in the planning for time lost due to holiday periods or other difficulties over dates e.g. factory closures, peak demand for seasonal items.

Budget for the costs involved in a tendering exercise such as printing, advertising, and professional advice.

Clearly establish who in your organisation has to be consulted about the product/service specification (did you hear about the new railway carriages that were too big for the tunnels?!) and who is responsible for making the final decision to place a purchase order. Research your exact requirements to an appropriate level of detail.

Collect the background information that will help potential suppliers, such as data about your organisation, your client, the overall aims of the project, details about previous years events (especially last year's), details of the plans for this year's event (dates, times etc.), information about any special considerations/policies (e.g. environmental requirements such as "only timber from renewable forests").

Identify potential suppliers (including current ones!) and the most appropriate means of advertising the tender. Where applicable, discuss your requirements directly with suppliers before the formal tender process starts especially where some form of close working relationship has to be established.

f) the specification

This element is obviously at the core of the purchasing process and key to its success. As the prospective purchaser you need to be able to describe exactly what your requirements are. (What, where, when, size, quality standard). The way this is done will vary according to whether you are specifying in respect of a product or a service or a sales concession.

In specifying you may express yourself in terms of the inputs you require, or the outputs you require or a mixture of the two. Here is a simplistic example to demonstrate the difference between inputs and outputs.

An input statement could be:

"The supplier to provide an ice cream sales point at each corner of the show field"

Whereas an output statement could be:

"The supplier to provide sufficient ice cream outlets to serve the needs of an expected visitor number of 5,000 visitors per day".

A mixture of inputs and outputs would be:

"The supplier to provide sufficient ice cream outlets to serve the needs of an expected visitor number of 5,000 visitors per day, subject to a minimum of four outlets".

The input statement is very clear. You say exactly what you require, making comparison of any bids based on this information easy to compare and easy to monitor thereafter. However it presumes that you are certain of your requirements.

If you were unsure as to how many ice cream outlets you needed, you might use the output statement and leave the bidder to assess what is required. This may, however, make it difficult to compare tenders between bidders offering different numbers of ice cream outlets and leaves open the question as to who is accountable if there are insufficient ice cream outlets to meet the demand during the event.

Specialist suppliers have extensive information and expertise which event managers need to use. Sometimes a formal tendering process seems to stand in the way of obtaining the most out of the partnership between client and supplier.

This is where output statements or pre-tendering discussions are very useful. For example "Supply and install appropriate security fencing for the event site" saves you researching a lot of detail but requires that the tendering process is sufficiently flexible for you to be able to ensure that a "cheap" bid that is not properly based does not beat the bid of an experienced firm working to trade organisation standards.

For long-term service contracts and series contracts a meaningful relationship with an appropriate partner is essential and very productive.

Beware of over-specifying, as that will cost you money through you paying for something that is not required or essential. Beware of duplication (or something falling through the net!) by ensuring that specifications for related products are comprehensive when viewed as a whole. (For example, if you specify "deliver to site", who is going to unload and erect?)

g) price and payment clauses

Specify when payments will be made to suppliers. These may be staged and dependent on progress as well as when a product is delivered. For example for some print and design work x% on appointment, y% on approval of design and copy, z% within four weeks of delivery of completed order.

Some payments may be offset by the supplier's opportunity to earn income as part of the contract or incentivised in some way. Ensure that whatever is proposed is capable of easy checking or auditing. For example a bonus payment/income share to an event organiser for attracting paying delegates to a seminar in excess of a specified number

Make provision for a basis on which contract variations can be negotiated. It is often the case that when organising an event that the original requirements are added to or amended. If the tender price is backed by a small schedule of rates then these rates can be used e.g. the charge out cost for additional time from particular grades of staff, or the price for attending additional meetings with the client over and above the number specified. Mileage and subsistence rates for additional travel might also be useful. Also valuable is a basis for re-charging additional items that the client asks the organiser to buy-in. That basis might be invoiced price plus a 5% handling fee.

Provide for accommodating price changes over time. Most contracts are fixed price but are for one off events or short-term activities. If the contract is for supply over an extended period e.g. organising an annual event for the next three years then contract clauses are required relating to how the quoted costs are to be varied over time. If there is no such provision then you may find yourself attracting higher than expected prices as suppliers ensure that they will recover future inflation in costs. If the prices quoted are too competitive then your

supplier might not be in business in three years time! If quoted prices are specified as moving in line with inflation be sure to quote which of the published inflation indices you are referring to. You might refer to different ones for example for fuel as compared with general inflation.

When purchasing services as opposed to goods there are a number of different options that can be used for the financial basis of the contract. It is unlikely that a simple quoted total cost will be a suitable arrangement.

These options include:

Management fee contract

The contractor tenders on the basis of receiving a fee for managing an activity. All income and expenditure is accounted for by the contractor and the balance is recharged (or in the case of a surplus – returned) to the client. The fee covers the contractor's costs and profit and may be supplemented by some form of incentive arrangement. This management fee option is often used where a client engages an event organiser to organise events on their behalf.

Concession

The concessionaire pays to exploit the concession on offer such as the right to organise events in a park over the season or the supply of a specialist product at an outdoor event (such as catering rights). The concessionaire is taking all the financial risk. The bid is the amount that the concessionaire will pay (and is normally paid prior to the event).

Lump sum contract

The contractor tenders on the basis of receiving a lump sum from the client with the opportunity for the contractor to use their expertise to earn additional income for themselves. This option enables an organisation to provide a service that normally costs them to provide e.g. an annual local authority show. The organisation limits its financial exposure to the lump sum and by providing this does not pass on an unrealistic financial risk to the contractor. The client retains some limited control by specifying some parameters to constrain the event organiser (not too many otherwise it becomes counterproductive!).

Schedule of rates

The supplier will be paid using the rates according to the actual amount of work required e.g. fencing or cabling. Often used in construction and landscaping contracts where the total amount of work is uncertain at the outset e.g. reinstatement of ground after an event. It will usually be subject to a minimum contract payment.

h) tender documents

The documents you require will include:

- advertisements inviting expressions of interest in the contract
- pre-qualification questionnaires to obtain basic information from prospective bidders
- specification
- Terms and Conditions of Contract
- Terms and Conditions of Tendering
- bid document
- pro-forma contract including schedule of rates (if applicable)

i) selecting and evaluating tenders

The first issue to be dealt with is - are the firms that are submitting tenders well established (relative to the size and duration of the contract) and do they meet all the criteria set out in the terms of the tender? This may have been established by judging firms at the 'pre-qualification' or 'expression of interest stage'. Clearly, if a firm has been accepted at these prior stages it cannot be subsequently rejected on the grounds that it is not properly established! Subsequently the issues are of price and quality.

To evaluate the bids the full bid price has to be established from the bid documents – hopefully they are constructed so that the full price is clearly stated! Where method statements and other information has been asked for this has to be assessed preferably against previously published criteria.

j) awarding the contract

Once the winning bid or tender has been identified it is often necessary to have a discussion with the successful tenderer. The purpose being to ensure that the tenderer is still interested in making the supply at the price quoted, and in order to clarify any detailed requirements. (Post tender discussions on price are a difficult area and beyond the scope of this publication).

The order can then be placed. This will require the documentation to be drawn up and completed by both sides at the initiative of the client. An official written order may suffice or a contract may have to be drawn up. It is essential that this is done without delay as it is unfair and leads to problems if a supplier is asked to start work in advance of receiving a written order/contract.

k) monitoring the contract

Once the contract or order has been placed remember that that is not the end of the process, but the beginning! Check with the supplier in the period before supply takes place to ensure that all is going according to plan. When supply takes place, check that the goods are as ordered or check that ongoing services are operating successfully. If things are not right enter into discussion with the supplier as soon as possible.

Looked at like this purchasing can be seen to be very complicated. It's up to you to keep the level of complexity in line with the nature of the purchasing that you are doing. Over complication always leads to financial inefficiencies. Too simplistic an approach may produce a satisfactory financial outcome but leave you at best disappointed and at worst unable to fulfil you event's requirements and exposed to significant liabilities.

Mike Fulford, Consultant with Leisure Advice, supplied this section on procurement and his details can be found in the back of this book.

chapter seven

marketing

Unless your event is totally unique and everybody already knows about it then marketing is essential if your event is to be successful. Marketing is not just about promotion (an additional section on this later); it is about trying to deliver an event product that the customers want at an affordable price and then making sure they know about it.

Competition for the leisure pound is immense and therefore potential customers have to be persuaded to buy into your event. Your event is NOT going to appeal to everyone. It will appeal to a certain type of customer who has the potential to be interested in attending. It is critical to identify this target group of customers and then communicate with them in terms which will appeal mostly to them.

a) the marketing mix

Effective marketing is about creating a successful marketing mix – getting the right blend of a variety of components – to ensure that an enjoyable and attractive event is delivered for customers. This blend is about considering carefully each of the following 'Ps' and delivering them appropriately for any specific event. The main Ps are:

Product   the quality event

Place   a suitable venue

Price   considered, set and packaged

Promotion   raising awareness

Programming   fitting into an activity and/or a calendar

Packaging   fitting together with other activities/events/projects

People   the key delivery factor

b) the marketing strategy

The preparation of a marketing strategy is essential to any successful event and should take account of the planning and budgetary planning timetables. Your strategy should include:

i) **a mission statement**
(what is your ultimate vision for the event?)

Here is an example mission statement:

- To provide a high profile festival for the community of Anytown and surrounding areas which will satisfy audience requirements and meet the aspirations of the Council and the Community.

ii) **an audit** – who will the event appeal to?

With regard to 'audience building' you will need to research the various social classes within the event catchment area (ie classes A, B, C1, C2, D and E). You will need to find out:

- age
- sex
- occupation
- means of transport
- distance willing to travel to event

iii) **analysis** (strengths, weaknesses, opportunities and threats – SWOT).

Clearly identify what it is about your event that will appeal to the target audience. eg;

Strengths
- existing loyal event attenders
- good access to site
- ample car parking facilities
- experienced organising staff
- organisation improves every year
- high level of technical management
- good health and safety track record

Weaknesses
- no undercover/wet weather facilities on site
- lack of 'branding'
- limited marketing resources
- diverse range of elected members' priorities

Opportunities
- could cater for specialist groups

- opportunities to create mailing lists for next year (data capture)
- partnerships with (other) local authorities
- have a 'give 'em what they want' policy
- use the USP (Unique Selling Proposition) of the event, eg type of audiences, size of event, geographical position, welcoming atmosphere, attendance of celebrity/royalty
- attracting sponsorship
- build relationships with relevant agencies such as Regional Arts Boards, etc
- maximisation of secondary income opportunities (sales of souvenir programmes/catering/merchandising)
- introduction of new market sectors

Threats
- similar event in neighbouring areas
- other local events with different pricing policies, especially 'free' events
- difficult economic climate (possibly within the organisation)

iv) aims and objectives

(as outlined in the Events section in Chapter One)

v) the plan

(tactics, budget, sponsorship)
see various chapters relating to these items

vi) implementation

(who does what, when and how)

The strategy should be a working document used by all involved in the event and actioned by all individuals who are allocates specific tasks. The strategy should be monitored, updated and rewritten whenever necessary. The following activities should be paramount:
- programming policy
- pricing levels/structures
- pricing differentials
- incentives
- promotion
- distribution
- daily monitoring of ticket sales (for more information on ticketing see Chapter 13 (b) – Other Event Components)

Reviewing the event is just as important as planning and implementation. Achievements should be recorded:

- box office income
- secondary income
- grants
- donations
- sponsorship
- customer satisfaction
- audience development
- new markets gained
- staff performance
- on-site management
- pre-event and on-site public relations
- promotion
- monitoring and review (post event – what worked, what could be improved)

c) promotion and publicity

An event is, of course, much easier to promote if it is already established as an important event. If it has a history of being well organised and has a high degree of audience and staff loyalty, this provides an excellent base from which to market your event.

d) publicity tactics

Listed below is a number of tried and tested publicity tactics highlighting a number of marketing opportunities, particularly with regard to promotion, ticket sales and public relations. This list is meant to stimulate the thought processes for maximising sales opportunities, improving public image and to assist in staging a high profile event.

- stage a press call and provide some hospitality
- ensure programme caters for specialist groups
- give out free promotional items in advance to advertise the event
- develop relationships with national and local press, radio, television, trade press outside as well as within catchment area
- do leaflet drops/mailshots directly to homes (if an envelope is used, sell space in the envelope to a local company who may wish to advertise – this will offset any mailing charges)
- negotiate eight-page colour pull-out supplement with the local newspaper or use the 'wrap around' method
- contact TV production companies to create a behind-the-scenes documentary (or produce a storyboard with the same theme for newspapers)
- engage a high profile celebrity/crowdpuller to attend press

calls talk to the public about their views on the event

- involve a charity with a high profile patron
- use sponsors' names as frequently as possible in publicity material
- always use photographs with press releases, they usually attract more attention than text
- use local colleges/universities' art departments to design posters/brochures, etc
- advertise on taxis and buses
- tie in with your local newspaper to run a competition using the phrase 'using your skill and judgment' (but remember that any special promotions, such as competitions, should last for ninety days only)
- use display boards in public buildings, eg leisure centre, library, civic centre
- persuade shopkeepers to stock brochures and display posters, offer an incentive such as two free tickets to the shopkeeper
- link the event to an anniversary
- set up a distribution network for your leaflets in tourist information centres, libraries, local hotels, colleges, doctors and dentists surgeries, hairdressers, restaurants, pubs, schools etc .
- erect banners

e) corporate image

A corporate image creates instant associations in the minds of potential customers. It is especially important for your targeted customers to understand and appreciate what your event stands for and the corporate image is vital to get right. Thus, every time you communicate with somebody you create an impression of your organisation. Everything you commit to paper therefore will dictate somebody's perception of your event. A clear corporate image for your event will save time, money and effort in addition to generating a greater response to your work. It will ensure a consistent and professional identity to all who come into contact with it.

Everything that is associated with the corporate image for the event should be associated with quality. You can spend less time worrying about what your print job will look like if you work within the corporate image guidelines.

Think about what you want to say, how you are going to present it and how it could be improved. Think about everything you print. Talk to your design team, provide a full brief on how you want your material to look.

f) theme

A theme provides a brand for the event and is the most visible aspect of marketing. It can:

a   create a high profile image which is distinctive and memorable

b   encourage high levels of participation

c   assist in attracting sponsorship, donations and gifts

d   raise the profile of an area and its residents

To make the theme work it must be understood that this is only a part of the whole marketing mix. Organisers will need to ensure that they create a logo which is in line with the theme and which is instantly recognisable. It should be applicable to a wide variety of situations, particularly to publicity material.

g) media relations

It is all too easy to complain about lack of coverage in the press and other media for our events. We all have it in our hands to improve the situation. You must cultivate relationships with your local media. Work hard on this area since ultimately the local media can bring you massive publicity benefits and awareness (for FREE!).

Here are a few pointers worth following to help in dealing with the media. With these suggestions and your own ideas and initiatives, you may have some success in obtaining the coverage your event deserves:

- be professional at all times
- be reliable – send whatever information you promised
- be punctual – deadlines are crucial to journalists
- be accurate – no-one likes to publicise erroneous information
- be friendly – work hard to cultivate relationships with media contacts
- be first – the 'first' of anything is news
- be controversial – the media want 'news', not necessarily 'bad' news
- be well presented – a clear press release, properly presented and issues is essential
- be personal – follow up by phone call to journalists you have circulated if you have further information to give
- be visual – a good picture is worth a lot of words to readers, journalists and sponsors
- be innovative – new ideas are more likely to get coverage
- be interesting – feature the unique, or most novel, aspect of your event in your press release headlines
- be positive and enthusiastic – your attitude will affect that of the media: enthusiasm is infectious

There is no magic remedy or guarantee of success but following these guidelines – thinking them through on each occasion – will help get better coverage.

Remember local media will be keen for your information, but national, less so. You have to work harder for the bigger coverage.

Good media coverage adds to an event in many ways – for spectators, officials, sponsors and participants. It makes all the effort worthwhile if many people are interested.

The following are key points in maintaining good media relations and ensuring that media coverage is obtained for events:

- plan activities well in advance and keep the media informed
- make direct contact with the editor and specialist journalists to discuss potential coverage for events
- be precise in details provided to the media of future plans
- build up stories around personalities, local and national
- pick out local elements of national stories for local media outlets
- don't be put off if initial attempts at local or national coverage do not succeed – discuss these matters with the editors and be persistent in pursuing them and coming up with new ideas
- supply copies of forthcoming events lists to magazines and newsletters which circulate within the media
- include photographs whenever possible
- don't simply concentrate on specialist features or journalists. Arts, sports or tourism, for example, can justify coverage in general features, as well as news and current affairs slots
- be professional in your approach at all times and study the relevant advice and publications to retain up-to-date knowledge of the media and how to approach them
- use of other relevant agencies, like Arts Councils or Sports Councils publicity mechanisms to add to your own
- have a recognised event or promotion contact for the media rather than a diverse range of people giving diverse views. The personal touch is very important for all concerned
- remember there are many forms of media: all want information so try to utilise them all. There cannot be too much information being pumped into the media to allow them to plan coverage.

Make sure that you provide the media with information and situations with which they can work. The following is a list of tactics which could be used to attract the attention of the media:

- stage a press call for an event launch. The first exposure for the event should be a press release, sufficiently early to ensure that the information allows time for newspapers, magazines and newsletter deadlines
- a photocall should be arranged to coincide with this release, featuring performers and the organisers
- invitations to the photocall should be restricted to press representatives, key council representatives (if appropriate) and sponsors
- staging the press call outdoors will stimulate the interest of passers-by and create some local publicity
- in order to ensure press coverage, develop human interest stories and features with photographic support
- create a co-ordinated publicity programme for the event including the media and advertising
- give special emphasis to securing coverage in local and regional media within a thirty-mile radius (if it is a 'local' event)
- produce an event newsletter
- produce a supplement for inclusion in the local newspaper
- publicise information about concessionary tickets

h) advertising

Well-targeted, cost-effective advertising can be the difference between success and failure for events. It is also an important matter to consider the costs involved in placing advertisements. You must be clear about your objectives and who your target market is.

There is a wide range of advertising vehicles available, for instance:

- newspapers
- magazines
- newsletters
- poster sites
- buses/taxis
- railway stations
- radio/television
- ceefax/teletext
- direct mail (door to door)
- school noticeboards
- surgeries (doctors, dentists, etc)
- cinemas
- underground
- reverse side of car parking tickets
- other public places such as leisure centres, hairdressers, colleges, etc
- internet

The usual types of advertisements appearing in newspapers or magazines take the usual formats:

- wrap-around (local newspaper)
- double-page spread
- full page colour
- full page mono (black and white)
- half page colour
- half page mono
- quarter page colour
- quarter page mono
- spot colour (a single colour added for a small charge)
- classified
- earpiece (usually in the form of a small strip designed diagonally across the corner of a newspaper)

The cheapest form of advertising is if you are successful in persuading the local newspaper to sponsor your community event which usually results in free or very low cost advertising.

i) promotions

Promotions can work exceptionally well with 3rd party partners. Promotions are special offers to selected customers to enable them to buy into your event. Here are a few examples to consider:

- tie in a special offer with a local supermarket especially for their customers
- tie in an exclusive promotion with your local radio station/newspaper
- can you offer schools special promotions?
- the emergency services, colleges and universities could be targeted with special promotions to reach their audiences.

j) exhibitions/roadshows

Creating exhibition stands and going on a local 'roadshow' in your towns/villages is an excellent way of creating awareness. Obviously it costs money to create graphics to display on exhibition boards. However many graphics can be blown up to large scale to exhibit at reasonable prices. Your exhibition, which ought to be staffed during peak hours, can go on display at local sports centres, shopping malls, stations, etc.

k) printed material

i) brochures

Event brochures should contain:

- the title of the event
- the subject
- who should attend and why
- the intended participants and spectators
- where and when the event will take place (including a map showing how to find the venue)
- the outline programme
- cost, what it covers and payment terms
- how to register, including a registration form or ticket application
- essential administrative details (eg timings, travel and accommodation)
- any special terms and conditions (cancellation charges, discount schemes, etc)
- the name, address and telephone number of the organising body along with the company name, registered number and address. It is also useful to give the VAT number
- disclaimer notice (usually in the form 'the organisers reserve the right to make such changes to the programme as may be necessary due to conditions outside their control')

ii) direct mail

Direct mail is a useful method of creating awareness of your event. Once your publicity material (brochure) has been printed, direct mail can ensure it goes to the people most likely to be interested in the event.

If you cannot afford to buy database of potential customers (there are many list brokers to try such as www.MarketingFile.com), then you could include the leaflet with your local newspaper. The Royal Mail can deliver your brochure to individual homes, but this can be expensive.

If you can send your leaflet out with a 3rd party's material this may be more cost effective. Partners such as your local council, utility companies and other major employers in the area could be approached.

l) press releases

Journalism has been called 'literature in a hurry' and that analysis will be endorsed 100% by editors who have to sift through mountains of press releases, produce stories and meet deadlines.

Remember, hard-pressed editors have a VERY SHORT attention span. If the first sentence of your press release doesn't grab their attention and give them an idea of what follows on, they will file it in the waste paper bin. It is so important to ensure that your first sentence 'hooks' the editor. If it interests him/her it will probably interest the reader. By providing well written press releases which require the minimum of sub-editing, you are increasing the chances of event news being published or broadcast.

However, there is no guarantee your news will be printed but don't give up – keep trying. Editors will always respond to a local news source who submits good, clear copy on time. Establishing a working relationship with the local media will ensure that your event is covered.

Press coverage – why do we want it?

- increases awareness of the event
- encourages new participants, spectators, audiences and is fuel to sponsorship
- lets general public know about the event
- assists in attracting sponsorship and general interest
- gives existing sponsors good publicity
- influences funding authority

Here are some general rules for putting together press releases. Perhaps you may consider the criteria too involved and detailed but don't forget that this is the newspaper game and you have to play by their rules.

Setting out a press release

- use A4 paper typed on one side only where possible
- double-spaced with wide margins
- have a half- to one-inch margin on either side of the page
- dated
- include event contact name, address and telephone number, email, fax number and website
- embargo date – which delays publication – if necessary
- make sure it is submitted BEFORE the publication's print deadline

Key points to cover

- answer the questions: who, what, where, when, why and how
- keep length of the first sentence to NO MORE THAN 20 words and keep following sentences as short and snappy as possible
- never start press releases with the words THE, THAT or THIS
- make sure details – dates, names and times – are correct
- don't use flowery language, clichés or jargon
- if copy goes onto further pages, write MORE at bottom of

each completed page and END below the last sentence of press release

- NEVER run sentences from one page to the next
- don't underline anything
- be topical

Content

- Always date your press release
- Don't forget your contact name and number. If the editor wants to follow up the story he/she will need to get back to you quickly. If you have a home and a business number, give both
- Headlines: the best way to learn to write headlines is to pick up a paper and go through the leadlines in it, looking at the style. Try to think what the essence of your story is and then express it in five words or under. Make your headlines witty, give them some sort of impact. They are the first thing which readers will notice, and if your headline doesn't attract their attention they will not read your story
- Introduction: once again, if your introduction is not gripping, no one is going to read the rest of the story. As in the case of headlines, try to think of the essence of your article and the most exciting way of presenting it
- Paragraphs: you must write in paragraphs for newspapers and you must put your paragraphs in order of importance of the subject matters they contain
- Style: the actual result and an accurate account are of less interest than the human interest story. Put the event into context. Try to get pertinent quotes from key event parties
- Avoid writing technical details that would baffle the ordinary reader. Write what is termed 'journalese' and is the normal language you see written in reports. Editors do not appreciate flowery English. Journalese crams as much information into the fewest possible words

m) marketing and promotions checklist

- appoint advertising agency
- compile programme of events
- establish logo
- register logo
- print logo guidelines
- create campaign with direct mail/personal selling, telephone sales
- compile advertising schedule
- produce public relations strategy
- identify opportunities for sales promotion
- consider most economical/effective packaging

- compile a signage schedule for venues
- keep a film and book record of the event
- produce regular event update publicity
- consider commemorative coins/stamps
- consider radio/tv advertising
- produce maps for the event
- order flags and banners
- order merchandising items, ie pins, ties, badges, caps, etc
- consider a requirement for medals/certificates for volunteers
- consider hospitality arrangements for sponsors
- are there to be any displays/exhibitions?

Appreciation is expressed to David James of Arena Marketing, for contributing to this chapter. His contact details are listed at the back of this book.

"An expert is someone who knows some of the worst mistakes that can be made in his subject and who manages to avoid them"   *Werner Helsenberg 1901–76*

chapter eight

event safety management

Health and safety is of paramount importance. It is essential to look after all those personnel involved in an event, whether they are employees (including volunteers) contractors and also members of the public. Health and safety is closely linked with quality management. Many organisers regard health and safety as a bureaucratic, paper-producing exercise and either don't bother at all or produce volumes of sometimes irrelevant paperwork, which is of no use at all.

a) legislation

The main health and safety legislation is covered by the Health and Safety at Work Act 1974 (HASAWA) and there is a great deal of information around on its requirements. In essence, it makes it a legal responsibility for employers to ensure that all work activities are safe for those that use them. Events are classed as work activities, whether or not they are in purpose-built venues, greenfield sites, streets, etc. Their legal responsibility covers all persons working on or visiting the event. The Act is criminal law; a failure to do so can result in statutory action leading to the serving of notices, fines and/or imprisonment. It is controlled by the concept of "reasonably practicable".

"Reasonably practicable" is often described by association with a pair of scales, one scale carrying "risk" the other time, cost, trouble and physical difficulty. If the scale containing "risk" goes down, it is heavier (or highly likely) then the other part of the scale goes up (whatever the time, cost, trouble is less important than the probability of injury, damage or loss). In legal terms, if the quantum of risk exceeds the time, trouble, cost, technical knowledge and physical difficulty of carrying out the duty then the control or protective measure must be carried out or installed, irrespective of the financial position or size of the employer's company.

The skill is getting the balance right. Guidance on health and safety standards can be found in the Event Safety Guide (Purple Guide/Pop Code), an HSE publication.

Self-employed persons also have a legal responsibility to undertake their work activities in a safe manner. In addition, employees are legally obliged to act in a safe way and adhere to safe methods of work and not to endanger their or others' health and safety.

Many organisers believe that strict standards should be available for their events so that they can easily know what is required. This is somewhat short-sighted and does inhibit the creativity that is required for events to progress, in order to stimulate and satisfy future audiences. All events are unique and are a combination of venue, entertainment and audience profile. Consequently, each event requires its own unique safety standards, which often are, in themselves, innovative and creative. We need to comply with the law but it should not inhibit our creativity. This is why risk assessments are such a useful and creative tool.

b) risk assessment

Risk assessment is a term often used, a term which is often misunderstood and believed by some to be yet another bureaucratic, paper producing exercise. Let's examine the concept in more detail in relation to events.

Under the Management of Health and Safety at Work Regulations 1999 it is a legal requirement for the employer or self-employed person to ensure that risk assessments are carried out at their work places/activities. This should be suitable and sufficient and carried out by a competent person. Other legislation covering noise, manual handling, etc also require risk assessments but are beyond the scope of this chapter.

A suitable and sufficient risk assessment is one that:

* correctly and accurately identifies a hazard
* disregards inconsequential risks and those trivial risks associated with life in general
* determines the likelihood of injury or harm arising
* quantifies the severity of the consequence and the number of people who would be affected
* takes into account any existing control measures
* identifies any specific legal duty or requirement relating to the hazard

- will remain valid for a reasonable amount of time
- provides sufficient information to enable employers to decide upon appropriate control measures, taking into account the latest developments and advances
- enables employers to prioritise remedial measures

Records of assessments must be completed and held where five or more persons are employed. It is good practice to always do this.

To recap, we need appropriate site design, appropriate safety measures and standards and competence tailored to suit the event. Under or over provision can cost time, money and, of course, lives. The combination of venue, event and audience profile is totally unique. Specific standards are required, standards which are practical, pragmatic and workable.

The risk assessment approach is straight forward, but must be carried out by a competent person.

Under the Management Regulations, a competent person is "a person who has sufficient training and experience or knowledge and other qualities to assist the employer in securing compliance with the necessary legal requirements". The approved code of practice adds that who is considered a "competent person" depends on the situation and "does not necessarily depend on the possession of particular skills or qualifications", declaring "simple" situations may require only:

i)   an understanding of relevant current best practice;
ii)   an awareness of the limitations of one's own experience and knowledge.

The law appears to hedge its bets, allowing them to determine the case when necessary. The definition does, of course, vary according to the degree of hazards.

A truly competent person would know their limitations and know when to call in a professional.

c) the risk assessment process

A risk assessment establishes the likelihood of occurrence (ie chances that a hazard realises its potential to cause harm) multiplied by the severity of outcome (ie extent of injury, damage etc).

Risk = severity of outcome x likelihood of occurrence.

Risk can be presented numerically or alphabetically.

The first step is to identify the hazards –these are anything which has the potential to cause harm. A brainstorming session can be very useful, eg:

Alcohol	Audience
Chemicals	Electricity
Fire	Food hygiene
Ground conditions	Lack of competent contractors
Noise	Over capacity
Pyrotechnics	Unstable structures
Vehicle/Pedestrian Conflict	Water
Weather	Working at height

The next step is to identify those at risk, eg public, artistes, employees, contractors, venue staff.

Hazards identified should only be those that are thought to be significantly reasonably foreseeable ones.

We now need to assess the risk of each hazard having regard to the likelihood and severity. It is essential to carry out these assessments independently. It has been found that persons tend to let their judgement of the probability of events be influenced by the anticipated seriousness of the outcome.

The risk should be first evaluated with no contracts in place or existing contracts in place and then re-evaluated with the proposed contracts in place.

There are many ways of evaluating risk and there is no right or wrong way. Two such methods are shown below:

d) simple matrix

	High	Medium	Low	
High	3	3	2	**S**
Medium	3	2	1	**E V E R I T Y**
Low	2	1	1	
LIKELIHOOD				

Severity

High	=	Fatality – major injury causing long-term disability
Medium	=	Injury – an illness causing short term disability
Low	=	Other injury or illness

Likelihood

High	=	Certain or near certain
Medium	=	Reasonably likely
Low	=	Very seldom or never

Risk Rating

3	=	High risk
2	=	Medium risk
1	=	Low risk

e) detailed matrix

		SEVERITY					
		Multiple Death 10	**Single Death** 8	**Major Injury** 6	**'3 day' Injury** 4	**Minor Injury** 2	**None** 1
LIKELIHOOD	**Certain** 10	100	80	60	40	20	10
	Very Likely 8	80	64	48	32	16	8
	Probable 6	60	48	36	24	12	6
	Possible 4	40	32	24	16	8	4
	Unlikely 2	20	16	12	8	4	2
	Very Unlikely 1	10	8	6	4	2	1

Notes:

The numerical scale used is to allow comparisons of the risk levels only. No literal meaning is implied by the scoring level.

'Major Injury' shall be as defined in Reporting of Injuries, Diseases and Dangerous Occurrences Regulations.

Key to Shading

100	Level of risk is unacceptable.
24	Level of risk may be tolerable. Seek to reduce level of risk.
12	Level of risk is acceptable

Abbreviations used in assessments

P = Public
S = Staff
A = Artistes

Definition of likelihood classes

Certain	10	Has happened before and is expected to happen on this occasion
Very Likely	8	Has happened before and is very likely to happen on this occasion
Probable	6	Has been known to occur before and is likely to happen on this occasion
Possible	4	Has been known to occur before and it may happen on this occasion
Unlikely	2	Has been known to occur before but no reason to suggest that it will happen on this occasion
Very Unlikely	1	Has never happened before and there are no reasons to suggest it will happen on this occasion

The following pages contain examples of risk assessment documentation and a blank version which can be photocopied for your own use.

Subject area	Hazards and effect	To whom	Severity rating x likelihood = Primary risk based on no controls			Existing control measures	Severity rating x likelihood = Primary risk based on no controls			Action required where risks are not adequately controlled	Other comments
			S	x L	= R		S	x L	= R		
General arrangement of units, crowd movements, crowd flow and pinch points	**F1** Overcrowding/crushing	P	8	4	32	Site arrangements pre-planned and checked and approved by ESC (and HSE if appropriate). Spacing of units to be at least up to HSE guidance levels. Barriers to be used to prevent unauthorised access between closely spaced units where agreed.	4	2	8		
Hazards arising from rides/ activities themselves	**F2** Trips Falls Entanglement Collision	P	8	4	32	Reputable suppliers to be used. All rides to be checked in advance by ESC (and HSE if appropriate)	4	2	8		
Vehicle access	**F3** Collision	P	8	4	32	General road closures in effect. Delivery vehicles to be restricted to hours of fair closure.	2	2	4		
Generators	**F4** Fire/shock	P, S	8	4	32	Generator numbers to be reduced to a minimum. No petrol generators. Generators to be located in secure area. Fire fighting equipment to be provided. Electrical certification required before use and checked by ESC.	6	2	12		
LPG use	**F5** Fire explosion	P, S	10	4	40	LPG restricted to catering units. *See assessment for catering*	6	2	12		

Subject area	Hazards and effect	To whom	Severity rating x likelihood = Primary risk based on no controls			Existing control measures	Severity rating x likelihood = Primary risk based on no controls			Action required where risks are not adequately controlled	Other comments
			S	x L	= R		S	x L	= R		
Side shows	**F6** Ejection of materials/fire etc	P	6	4	24	Risk assessment for all side shows/street entertainers to be audited and agreed in advance by ESC.	4	2	8		
Alcohol use	**F7**	P, S	8	4	32	Policy required for operators and stewards on prohibition of alcohol use. Customers overly intoxicated to be refused admission in safety is likely to be compromised. Close co-ordination with police and stewards requested for operators if public disorder likely to occur.	6	2	12		
Power cables	**F8** Trips and falls	P, S	6	4	24	Minimise cable runs by grouping generators. Run cables in road gutters at back of rides where possible. Where cables pass over pedestrian routes cover with approved covers and locate in high visibility areas.	4	2	8		
Overcrowding	**F9** Lack of emergency access	P, S	10	4	40	Permanent secured emergency services access route at rear of rides through car parks. Areas large enough to allow crowd spread to allow vehicle access along main carriageway.	6	2	12		

Subject area	Hazards and effect	To whom	Severity rating x likelihood = Primary risk based on no controls			Existing control measures	Severity rating x likelihood = Primary risk based on no controls			Action required where risks are not adequately controlled	Other comments
			S	x L	= R		S	x L	= R		
Overcrowding	**F10** Crushing	P, S	10	4	40	Further details of rides footprints required together with ride capacities to determine if area large enough or numbers or rides to be reduced	8	2	16		
General environmental conditions	**F11** Trip/slip/fall	P, S	6	4	24	General conditions underfoot good, with some kerbs and some street furniture as trip hazards. Ensure lighting is adequate from existing streetlights and rides – check on back up street lighting power. Evaluate condition of surfaces – bad weather – salt as required in ice.	6	2	12		
Fire/bomb/ collapse of structure	**F12** Panic during evacuation overcrowding/ crushing	P, S	10	4	40	Installation of operation of fair arranged to reduce overall risk of incident occurring. Additional fire fighting equipment available. Adequate exit routes in place. Ensure proper close liaison with police and all parties to co-ordinate action. Ensure detailed evacuation plan in place for zone. Ensure proper communication in place between all parties and for public.	8	2	16		

Subject area	Hazards and effect	To whom	Severity rating x likelihood = Primary risk based on no controls S x L = R	Existing control measures	Severity rating x likelihood = Primary risk based on no controls S x L = R	Action required where risks are not adequately controlled	Other comments

Risk assessment matrices should be used with caution, proper thought should be given to the problems associated with each hazard and the most practical, pragmatic method in exercising control, otherwise it does become just a paper exercise. Used properly, you can achieve good safety standards and also analyse and achieve more exciting, challenging performances. New, diverse, unorthodox, exciting, challenging performance can be fully appraised and often made to work – essential if the industry is to move forward in a dynamic way.

Remember its what happens on site that matters, a mass of paper back at base is a waste of time.

Richard Limb of The Symonds Groups has written this section on Event Safety Management. You can find his contact details in the listings at the back of this book.

> "No man's knowledge here can go beyond his experience"
>
> *John Locke 1632–1704*

chapter nine

health and safety management

a) health and safety policy

The key elements of successful health and safety management should include:

- a health and safety policy
- plan to ensure policy is put into practice
- an effective structure and arrangements for delivery of the policy
- monitoring and reviewing performance

Each event should have a safety policy which demonstrates that the organisation accepts that concern for health and safety is an integral part of its set up, ie committed. It should include details of the organisation, roles and responsibilities and how the policy will be put into practice. The arrangements should cover the detailed matters, eg safe systems of work, access, egress, training, etc.

It is a legal requirement for employers employing five or more people to produce a written health and safety policy. The event organiser may be a person or organisation that promotes an event themselves, eg promoters, production companies, local authorities, it is likely that there will be more than five employees and, therefore, a written policy is a legal requirement.

b) health and safety planning

Health and safety planning is all about identifying, evaluating and controlling hazards and risks for whatever event – building, load in, the show, load out and breakdown.

This is best achieved by an Event Safety Plan. There are numerous ways of constructing such a plan, the following is a typical layout.

Venue Evaluation – contains detailed analysis of the venue, type, nature, location, capacity, etc.

Event Evaluation – what type of event is it? What is the audience profile? How does it interact with the venue?

Organisation and sub-contractors – contains details of

organisation structure, responsibilities and contractor details.

Event Health, Safety and Welfare – details of Event Safety Co-ordinator and policy statement

Generic and specific risk assessments

Following a risk assessment approach, details of:

- crowd management
- stewarding
- communication
- emergency procedures
- means of escape
- fire precautions and equipment
- noise control
- special effects
- medical
- temporary structures
- electrical services
- sanitary accommodation
- waste disposal

c) venue checklist

Pre-event planning

Event:			Date
Venue:			

No.	Aspect	Observation	Comment
1	Confirm venue capacity and ascertain if any limitations on use apply.		
2	Confirm that venue holds appropriate fire certificates and that fire appliances are available and suitable.		
3	Confirm arrangements for detection and raising alarm.		
4	Determine if venue can safely accommodate the event in respect of:		
	a) Anticipated numbers		
	b) Types of visitor		
	c) Traffic flow demands		
	d) Set design (floor loading, height restrictions, access etc)		
	e) Suspended items/rigging (weight restrictions, locations etc).		
5	Ascertain if any other event could result in conflict, excessive numbers or traffic control or noise problems.		
6	Are risk assessments available for all tied contractors (riggers, electricians, security etc)?		
7	Is a venue PS system in place for emergency announcements? How will this impact on pedestrians?		

Pre-event planning

Event:			Date:
Venue:			

No.	Aspect	Observation	Comment
8	Does the venue have first aid rooms/facilities? Are they available for use? Are they adequate?		
9	What arrangements are in place for access for:		
	a) Get in		
	b) Event days		
	c) Pull out		
10	Have all external contractors been requested to provide:		
	a) Details of participation?		
	b) Appropriate risk assessments?		
	c) Method statements covering construction, operation and removal of equipment?		
	d) Details of 'service' requirement, eg electrical supply, compresses air, access etc?		
11	From contract risk assessments have any special risks been identifies? If yes, have arrangements been agreed with venue?		
12	Have all contractors been provided with relevant health, safety, fire and emergency procedure information?		

Pre-event planning

Event:	Date
Venue:	

No.	Aspect	Observation	Comment
13	Have any arrangements been made to facilitate unloading of heavy and/or bulky items? (loading bay, fork lift, ramps, etc)		
14	Have schedules been planned to allow for shared workspace?		

Engineering services and facilities

No.	Aspect	Observation	Comment
15	Confirm availability of venue approved technical contact to ensure smooth use of services.		
16	Has a site plan detailing set build, seating arrangements, location of access and emergency exit routes been produced (plan may also identify electrical points, fire and first aid points, etc). Has it been passed by venue and Local Authority (if applicable)?		
17	Do any limitations exist on use of equipment, machinery or substances (smoke machines, pyrotechnics, etc)?		

Pre-event planning

Event:		Date	
Venue:			

No.	Aspect	Observation	Comment
Health and safety welfare			
18	Are adequate sanitary facilities in place for expected numbers?		
19	Are adequate facilities in place to provide refreshments for staff and contractors or are facilities available for external caterers?		
20	Has information about specific site features been issued to all participants (uneven ground, access routes, etc)?		
21	Has relevant personal protective equipment been ordered and distributed amongst staff (hi-vis jackets, gloves, harnesses, etc)?		
22	Determine venue's procedures and who to contact in event of:		
	a) Fire		
	b) Bomb or similar threat.		
	c) Ascertain assembly points and emergency vehicle approach routes and rendezvous points.		

This list has been prepared to assist you in both the planning of an event and to fulfil your obligations under the Health and Safety at Work Act 1974.

Completion of the forms alone does not imply that you have fulfilled all your obligations in law. However, used together with the relevant risk assessment form(s) will show that you have shown a "duty of care" and that you have taken all reasonably practicable measures to make your event as safe as possible.

Inspection completed by:..

Date:...

Further action required

Event:			Date	
Venue:				

No.	Action required	Actioned by	Date completed	Signed

d) health and safety check list

Pre-event planning

Event:			Date:
Venue:			

No.	Aspect	Observation	Comment
1	Have all contractors and participants been briefed in emergency arrangements including fire, bomb and first aid?		
2	Have all contractor's method statements and risk assessments been collated?		
Access and egress			
3	Are loading and unloading areas:		
	a) Clearly indicated?		
	b) Supervised?		
4	Are traffic areas (access/egress routes) clearly identified and supervised?		
5	Is access to the venue controlled? If yes, how are numbers present during build-up maintained?		
6	Is a system necessary/in place to ensure that only approved contractors are used?		
Fire and emergency planning			
7	Have adequate stewards and/or marshals been appointed?		
8	Have they been:		
	a) Briefed upon their role and fire, security and other emergency		
	b) Trained in use of fire extinguishers etc? Are records of such training held?		
9	Are all stewards, first aiders and exhibition controllers provided with effective means of communication with event controller?		

Pre-event planning

Event:		Date:
Venue:		

No.	Aspect	Observation	Comment
Fire			
10	Are fire lanes and emergency exits clearly identified?		
11	Are access routes/fire escapes etc clear of obstruction (cables, PA stands etc)?		
12	Are all fire appliances and exits detailed on site plan in place and serviceable?		
13	Are all fire, first aid and emergency exit signs visible from all sides?		
14	Have fire exits, fire alarm call points and fire fighting equipment been tested?		
15	Has the fire/venue technical officer approved site plans and inspected the site?		
First aid			
16	Have the first aiders been appointed and facilities been inspected?		
Control of material			
17	Are flammable materials, sources of ignition left unattended?		
18	Have arrangements been made to remove such materials from venue when not in use/ overnight?		
19	How are materials used controlled?		

Pre-event planning

Event:	Date:

Venue:	

No.	Aspect	Observation	Comment
Health and safety			
20	Identify location and suitability of skips, dustbins etc and programme for disposal of contents.		
21	Review arrangements to ensure all areas are kept clean and tidy.		
22	How often are bins emptied, floors swept, refuse collected?		
23	Are cleaning materials available for spills of paint or other liquids?		
24	Have adequate arrangements been made for removal and safe disposal of packaging and other waste material?		
25	Are these arrangements satisfactory?		
General site safety			
26	Are periodic walk arounds undertaken to ensure compliance with statutory requirements, venue/ organisers rules and that systems of work detailed within method statements are being followed? If yes, are non-compliance records kept? If yes, what follow up action is to be taken?		

Pre-event planning

Event:			Date:
Venue:			

No.	Aspect	Observation	Comment
Engineering services and facilities			
27	Have arrangements been confirmed for certification of electrical installations and other specialist supplies, eg compressed air? If yes, are these to the satisfaction of the venue?		
28	Have all 'services' been tested and certified prior to connection?		
29	Are copies of relevant certificates held by Project Office?		
30	Have any daily inspections or checks been specified as part of any certification? If yes, detail.		

Pre-event planning

Event:	Date:

Venue:

No.	Aspect	Observation	Comment
Pre-opening checks			
1	Is a formal inspection of all installations and venue facilities undertaken prior to opening? If yes, is this inspection undertaken jointly with venue specialist staff?		
2	Are safety tours undertaken prior to daily opening and periodically throughout the open periods? If yes, do tours of inspection include:		
	a) External areas to the exhibition halls?		
	b) All installations?		
	c) All access routes?		
	d) Registration area?		
	e) Concessions, including cafes and restaurants?		
	f) First aid rooms and toilets?		
	Are results recorded?		

Pre-event planning

Event:			Date:
Venue:			

No.	Aspect	Observation	Comment
Fire and emergency arrangements			
3	Have all participants, concession holders, venue and exhibition staff been briefed on fire and other emergency arrangements?		
4	Has the fire alarm been tested prior to opening?		
5	Are adequate numbers of stewards and/or marshals on duty? Are they at their post?		
6	Are fire lanes and emergency exits clearly identified?		
7	Are access routes/fire escapes etc clear of obstruction?		
8	Are all fire appliances detailed on site plan in place and serviceable?		
9	Are all fire, first aid and emergency exit signs visible from all sides?		
10	Has an external check of escape routes/fire exits been undertaken? Are all exits clear of obstruction? Is assembly point clear of obstruction?		
11	Are regular checks completed of any areas where smoking is permitted,or where installations or accumulation of refuse present a fire risk?		

Pre-event planning

Event:	Date
Venue:	

No.	Aspect	Observation	Comment
First aid			
12	Are the required numbers of first aiders on duty?		
13	Have first aid rooms been inspected and are records of injuries and treatment being made?		
Housekeeping			
14	Are the areas around bins and skips clean and tidy?		
15	Is there any indication that the arrangements for floor cleaning and emptying of bins are inadequate?		
16	How often are bins emptied and floors swept?		
17	Are those arrangements satisfactory?		
General site safety			
18	Are periodic walk arounds undertaken to ensure compliance with statutory requirements, venue/organiser's rules and that participants are only displaying/using approved products or material? If yes, are non-compliance records kept? If yes, what follow up action is to be taken?		

Pre-event planning

Event:			Date

No.	Aspect	Observation	Comment
Access and egress			
19	Are personnel with special needs (elderly, infirm, disabled etc) at event? If yes, have appropriate plans been made?		
20	Are reception areas and main traffic areas congested? If yes, is this excessive?		
21	Have measures been taken to ensure that it is not unreasonably difficult for any disabled person to access and enjoy the event?		

This documentation has been prepared to assist you in both the planning of an event and to fulfil your obligations under the Health and Safety at Work Act 1974.

Completion of the forms alone does not imply that you have fulfilled all your obligations in law. However, used together with the relevant risk assessment form(s) will show that you have shown a "duty of care" and that you have taken all reasonably practicable measures to make your event as safe as possible.

Inspection completed by: .... Date:

Pre-event planning

Event: | **Date**

Venue:

No.	Aspect	Observation	Comment

Further action required

Event:			Date	
Venue:				

No.	Action required	Actioned by	Date completed	Signed

e) event safety co-ordinator

It is good practice for all events to have access to competent help on health and safety issues. A competent person is someone who has sufficient training, expertise, experience or knowledge and other qualities that enable that person to devise and apply appropriate protective measures.

This function is normally undertaken by the appointment of an Event Safety Co-ordinator. Ideally, no other duties should be undertaken by this person.

Typical roles are:

1 liaise with lead sub-contractors, assist selection and monitoring.
2 assistance with inspection before and during the event.
3 checking of method statements and risk assessments.
4 preparing and monitoring of site safety rules.
5 checking appropriate certificates in respect of structures, electrical suppliers etc.
6 advise on unsafe work and the use of unsafe equipment.
7 communication of safety information to contactors on site.
8 monitoring and co-ordinating safety performance.
9 provision of advice on appropriate safety standards whilst on site.
10 co-ordinating safety in response to a major incident.

f) security and stewarding

The primary duty of all security staff is to ensure the safety, welfare and enjoyment of all customers and others attending an event. Security staff must treat all customers politely and with respect at all times. Staff should be sensitive to customers in distress or difficulty and assist them by referring them to welfare organisations on site when necessary. They must co-operate effectively with others working at the event and care must be taken to ensure that any action by security personnel is proportionate to the situation being dealt with and not to appear aggressive or 'over the top'.

Stewards are there to help rather than control, to make everyone's experience enjoyable.

Stewarding tasks may include:

- controlling parking
- marshalling traffic
- assisting police and other emergency services
- clearing litter
- fire patrolling
- patrolling areas in front of stage

- guarding barriers, gangways, exits and entrances
- backstage security
- dealing with minor incidents quickly and effectively with minimum disruption
- stewards must at all times respond quickly when help is required

Event organisers are advised to contact the British Security Industry Association to find out the latest information on security and stewarding issues, tel: 01905 21464 or www.bsia.co.uk.

i) responsibilities of the organiser

The event organiser is responsible for proper steward behaviour, in particular:

- the conduct of security staff
- briefing stewards as to their duties
- providing site plans
- providing code words for use in emergency situations
- providing sufficient rest and refreshments between shifts

g) welfare services

Welfare services provide a range of support for people attending events who find themselves in difficulty. The primary duty of all welfare staff is to alleviate the distress of people attending the event. They must treat people politely and with respect at all times and should be sensitive to people's needs.

The services must be available from when the event starts, until it closes at the end.

Welfare services at an event can be organised in a variety of different ways. At a small event, a single team may be responsible for the whole range of general welfare. More often, at larger events such as rock concerts, there will be a number of groups providing different services such as:

- information
- counselling
- befriending
- dealing with lost children
- helping people with drug problems
- lost/found property

Every welfare team must ensure as far as possible that the service which it offers is organised and presented so as to be appropriate and accessible to all persons who may be in need of it, and to facilitate equal access to it by all those attending the event, irrespective of age, sex, race, culture, religion, disability or sexual preference. There must be good communications between different welfare services and other providers of services on site, e.g. the organiser's team, stewards, first aid etc.

It is important to make sure that all welfare services are covered by insurance.

The following are examples of some welfare services which should be provided at all events:

i) information service

People attending events will ask for a wide variety of advice. The following are tips for dealing with typical enquiries made at an event:

Make a list of addresses and phone numbers of local services such as:

- banks/bureau de change/24 hour cashpoints
- chemists (including duty chemist over weekends)
- police station
- social services emergency number
- hospital with casualty department
- 24 hour garages
- bus station
- railway stations (and timetables)
- taxi firms
- bed and breakfast/guest houses
- Calor Gas suppliers
- camping shops
- public telephones

Have available:

- telephone directory
- Yellow Pages
- index box and cards for people to leave messages if they cannot find their relatives or friends on site
- gridded maps of the site showing all features, facilities and attractions, including arrangements for people with special needs
- event programme and timings
- name of events manager and how they can be contacted in an emergency
- have access to an outside line telephone for emergencies

ii) lost property

Report lost property to lost property office and police.

iii) found property

- keep records (index cards in categories of items)

- do not leave unattended
- do not accept left luggage
- take addresses of people handing in found property so that owner can thank them
- offer advice to report loss of credit cards to police
- do not let members of the public look in the lost property for a lost item
- ask for proof of identity and full description of property

iv) lost/found children

In this instance, lost children include teenagers under fifteen years of age. Helpers must sign a statement to the effect that they do not have any criminal convictions for offences relating to children and have been checked by the Criminal Records Bureau.

- remember to look after the parents as well as the children
- in the event of evacuation of the event site, take children with you
- keep a record of their details
- reassure the child
- never leave children unattended
- if you take a child anywhere (i.e. a visit to the toilet), tell other helpers and make a note of which child you are taking and where you are going
- alert the police and security, giving a full description of the child
- do not give food and drink (except water) as the child may have an allergy
- the parent/guardian must sign the record before the child is collected
- see chapter 14 (f) The Children Act 1989

Penny Mellor is a welfare consultant with many years events experience. Penny's details are listed at the back of this book.

h) insurance

Insurance protection for events is often one of the last things which organisers consider but is an essential ingredient of any event irrespective of size. Specialist insurers are available and can be contacted either directly or through an insurance broker.

Listed below are areas of cover to be considered, some or all of which may be relevant to a particular type of event.

1. Cancellation and abandonment

This type of cover is normally available so that it protects organisers against cancellations or abandoned events due to causes beyond their control although it is not possible to insure against lack of support for an event or financial failures. Examples of problems for event organisers are venues being unavailable at the last minute, bad weather, equipment failure, strikes and power cuts. Indoor events tend to pose less of a problem but with the development of the outdoor event industry in general, our ever-changing weather patterns can provide problems of their own. Organisers of outdoor events should consider the following:

- Pluvius (agreed value) cover – if an event is dependent upon admission fees from the public on the day, then even fairly light amounts of rainfall can affect income. Rain is therefore measured during the most important hours as far as the organiser is concerned ad, depending on the amount of rain that falls, a claim is made against the sum insured for the event. For example, an organiser whose gate opens at 10am in the morning may wish to insure the hours of 7am to 11am to protect those hours during which most visitors are expected to turn up.

i) legislation

Always remember that there can be legal differences between the countries of the United Kingdom, especially England and Scotland; there can also be specific local authority and bylaw differences.

It is always worth checking the details with appropriate local officials and enforcement agencies.

Richard Limb of The Symonds Group has written the section on Health and Safety Management in this chapter and his advice is very much appreciated. You can find his contact details in the listings at the back of this book

> "Don't clap too hard – it's a very old building"

John Osborne 1929

chapter ten

venue and site design

The general principle behind venue design is to provide an entertainment arena in which the audience can enjoy the entertainment in a safe and comfortable atmosphere with minimal impact on the general environment.

The requirement for certain safety provisions, the types, numbers and specifications of facilities/services will depend on the outcome of the risk assessment carried. The combination of venue, artiste and audience is a unique one and requires a bespoke approach. The final design of a site is the consequence of entertainment type, location, size and duration and as such it must integrate with the geographical, topographical and environmental infrastructure, the artistic concept of the promoter as well as achieving the appropriate safety and welfare provisions.

a) site suitability assessment

Before detailed site design criteria are addressed and actioned every site should receive a preliminary assessment to determine suitability. The main areas of concern are:

i) available space for audience, temporary structures, back stage facilities, car parking, camping, rendezvous point etc. Any site designer will already have a proposed capacity in mind, together with some ideas of the concept of the entertainment. Rough thumb nail calculations of the available space is useful at this stage.

ii) ground conditions - are they suitable? Even, well drained open sites are required. Steep slopes, boggy areas should be avoided.

iii) traffic and pedestrian routes and emergency access and egress - what routes already exist? Are they suitable to handle the proposed capacity? Is a separate emergency and exit possible? If not, can other routes be provided. Are roads, bridges etc structurally sound?

iv) position and proximity of noise sensitive buildings. Are there any nearby? Is it possible to satisfy both the requirements of the audience and the neighbours? A noise propagation test may be advisable. Too many sites have suffered from a lack of attention in this area. Make sure this can be accommodated.

v) geographical location - where is the site located? How far away is the hospital, fire station, public transport, facilities, car parking, major roads, the airport, etc? Such information can be valuable when assessing the suitability of the site and/or what extra facilities should be accommodated within the site?

vi) topography - How does the land lie in relation to its surrounding? Does it form a natural amphitheatre? Where does the sun rise and set? Could any natural features assist in noise alteration? Are there any natural hazards/features such as lakes and waterfalls?

vii) location and availability of services - water, gas, electric (including overhead cables), telephone, sewage. Are there any restrictions, hazards? Can they be used?

The above basic areas of concern can be easily addressed by walking the site. Study the appropriate mapping and seek advice and information from the local authority and venue management. Such information is valuable and essential for commencing detailed site design. For existing venues much of this information may be available from the venue management and/or local authority.

b) pre-design data collection and appraisal

The next step in site design is to collect all the available data together and appraise it. Both the risk and the site suitability assessments will have produced valuable information upon which the site design will be based. The following information should now be at hand:

i) proposed occupant capacity

ii) artiste profile

iii) audience profile

iv) duration and timing of event

v) venue evaluation

vi) promoters concept and vision – artistic nature of event, single stage, multiple arena complex

The above information is then used to calculate what provisions/facilities are required to be accommodated within the site, ie, stages, tents, barriers, toilets, first aid, accommodation, concessions, exits, entrances, hospitality area, site lines, power, water, sewerage, gas, delay towers, perimeter fencing, facilities for the police, backstage requirements, viewing platforms, waste disposal requirements, etc.

Once all the information is collated detailed site design can commence.

c) site plans

Initial site design should ideally arise from a rough sketch on a site plan resulting from a detailed examination of the plan and an intimate knowledge of the site. Once the basic outline has been determined detailed scaled site plans should be produced. Often, many versions may exist as amendments are made on a new site, these could be as many as 10. The final site plan may be only finalised a few days before the show.

d) venue capacity/occupant capacity

The capacity of a venue is generally dependant upon the free available space for persons and the number of emergency exits available for use. The latter being the subject of a calculation involving the appropriate evacuation rate, ie width of available exit space and appropriate evacuation route.

Free available space is that space not taken up by non-occupant structures, which affords a view of the entertainment, whether direct or otherwise. In venues where seating is provided the major part of the occupant capacity will be determined by the number of seats available. However, in other cases a calculation based on the acceptable occupant density should be carried out. Generally 0.5m2 per person is used.

Capacity calculations for each individual area of entertainment should be made, ie each tent, room, arena etc. The overall capacity being the sum of the individual parts, subject to final perimeter fence access/place of safety calculations, ie note it may not be necessary to leave the site to gain a place of safety, eg large parks.

e) exit requirements

The exit numbers for a venue depend directly on the occupant capacity and the appropriate evacuation time for the type of structures. The publications "Guide to Safety and Sports Grounds" and "Guide to Fire Precautions in Existing Places of Entertainment and Like Premises" give details which relate to stadia and fixed entertainment premises including sample calculations. For open air events an evacuation time of fifteen minutes is generally acceptable. Evacuation rates relate to the

time it takes to reach a place of safety – this may not necessarily mean through exits to the outside of the venue, eg outdoor parking. It is worthy to note that, according to research, that eighty persons can move through a 1m gap in 1 minute.

f) exit position

Exits should be strategically placed evenly around the perimeter and be clearly visible whether directly or indirectly by signage. They should be free from obstruction on either side, ie information boards, catering concessions, meeting points etc should be kept away (at least 6m). The final exit terminus should be assessed and to be as safe as possible, ie, open into open spaces, assembly areas rather than main road/traffic flows. Wheelchair access should be taken into consideration. Ideally exits for pedestrian and service/concession vehicles should be separate. The exit gate should be able to operate efficiently and effectively. Careful consideration should be given to their siting.

NB: The preliminary occupant capacity calculation and exit requirements should be double checked once all initial infrastructure requirements/facilities are in place on the site design.

g) venue access

Venue access is a function of the design and location of transport and parking facilities and the design of access roads. Such facilities should be able to cope with the peak demand as determined from the arrival profile. The layout of the access routes will obviously depend upon the location of the facilities. Ideally, the roles should be spread around the site to minimise the load. Such routes should not converge down a single path and should be simple, easy and direct. Cross flows should be avoided.

h) entrances

The entrances provide the means for supervising, marshalling and directing the audience to the event. At some venues they may be used as an exit, at others such as a football stadium they are separate.

The design and location of entrances involved determine the numbers of entrances required where they should be and the capacity to be handled at each entrance.

There should be efficient numbers of entrances to cope with the peak demand and should achieve a smooth and orderly flow of people through them. The direction from which people are likely to come, the maximum number of people from each direction and the flow rate through the entrance are important issues which determine the number of entrances required. For purpose built venues these will already have been considered and approved. Flow rates depend on the type, design and width of the entrances, together with whether or not searching takes place. Flow rates can vary from 60 persons per minute without searching per 0.5m exit width to 6 with complete search. (The "Green Guide" gives flow rates applicable to sports stadia).

Consideration should also be given to the desired entry time (the time taken to allow all access to the venue which will depend entirely upon the type and duration of the event and the annual profile. The possibility of inclement weather may affect the desired time.

Any queuing systems to manage the crowd will need to be accommodated and taken into the calculations.

Flow through entrances:

$$= \frac{\text{width of element (m) x flow rates x time}}{0.5}$$

i) sight lines and video screens

The main concept behind venue design is to maximise the enjoyment of the public whilst effectively controlling crowd density and dispersal. It is important that the audience has a clear line of vision to the stage in order to avoid movement towards the centre. The widest possible sightlines from stage right to stage left help to reduce crowd density in front of the stage and help to minimise surging and the possibility of crushing injuries. The stage width, height and position of PA wings etc all affect sight lines. Sight lines should be engineered to create areas of space on the immediate stage left and right. This allows emergency/access movements.

All infrastructure items such as catering concessions, wc's etc should, where possible, be located outside the sight triangle.

For very large audiences the increased distances between the stage and the "back row" makes for poor sight lines and reduced entertainment value. This can lead to crushing and overcrowding. Strategically placed video or projection screens can be very effective. Screens located at some distance from the stage can encourage a proportion of the audience to move to a less crowded part of the site. Screens near the stage can help to stop people pushing towards it. Not all types of screen operate in daylight and if the intention is to use a screen in these conditions it will be necessary to ensure that an appropriate type is used.

Such screens may require substantial foundations and support and space and should be allowed for in any site design.

j) seating arrangements

Where an event is likely to attract an audience which is predominantly under the age of 16 there is a risk of over excitement leading to hysteria. The organiser should consider holding an all-seated event as this may help to prevent crowd surges and crushing at the front of the stage area spacing requirements and aisle widths etc can be found in the "Yellow Guide".

If temporary seating is provided, it will be necessary to ensure that the seating is adequately secured to avoid "snaking". The provision of loose seats is not recommended unless the seating area is very small.

k) slopes

When venues have slopes in excess of 1 in 6, consideration should be given to the provision of exit steps or ramps with a non-slip surface. The area in front of the stage should be as flat as possible in order to prevent tripping and crushing.

l) observation points

At some major outdoor concerts observation points may be considered necessary. These should be strategically placed to maximise the "view". Safe access and egress should be established.

m) production infrastructure/backstage requirements

The production infrastructure will depend very much on the type, size and duration of the event. Typically production offices, refreshment facilities, accommodation (for crew artists), dressing rooms, storage space, equipment, needs to be accommodated, usually backstage. Careful consideration should be given to the number of units required, fire hazards, access routes and circulation space, generators, first aid posts, ambulance/fire/police requirements. Large events may have several hundred working personnel.

Artiste areas should be kept separate from production/working areas and need to be thought out. Vehicles and pedestrian routes should be kept separate where possible.

n) fire and ambulance requirements

Fire and ambulance requirements all depend upon a risk assessment approach. The requirement, ie parking areas, first aid posts, rendezvous points, triage areas etc need to be carefully assessed and positioned in the appropriate places. The site should be designed so that they are readily accessible. Fire appliances should be able to access all parts of the site and be able to get within 50m of any structure. For wet, difficult ground, temporary roading may be necessary.

Emergency access routes should be established and agreed with the relevant authorities. These should be kept free at all times. Separate gated access/egress should be considered.

o) police and stewarding positions

The presence of police and the number of positions of stewards will depend upon the nature and type of entertainment provided and as such a risk assessment approach will be required. For large events a significant number of personnel will be on site, together with support/welfare facilities such as catering, wc's, showers, offices, search facilities, sleeping accommodation and control units. Such facilities may form a separate compound or be distributed between backstage and/or main entrance area. Such requirements should be carefully evaluated and incorporated into the site design.

p) hospitality area

The level of hospitality will vary with the size of the event and the organisers/artistes wishes. Accommodation and facilities may need to be provided for only a handful of persons requiring no more than a small meeting area through to very large sophisticated complexes catering for several thousand people. Marquees and viewing platforms may be required. The exact requirements should be agreed and designed for. Often such large numbers are forgotten in the capacity calculations and should be included.

q) noise considerations

The overall site design and layout should seek to maximise public enjoyment and protect the neighbours from noise nuisance. Careful consideration should be given to the stage location and other sound sources, having regard to nearby noise sensitive properties and the topography of the site. Slopes and natural barriers should be used to their maximum effect. It may well be advantageous to use a distributed sound system suspended from delay towers. Careful consideration should be given to the siting and construction of such towers in order to control site lines, crushing points and unauthorised "viewing" platforms.

r) catering and merchandising concessions

The number and type of concessions found at any event is largely dependent upon the commercial viability of such an event. The Mobile and Outside Caters Association gives guidance on appropriate provision. Such concessions may be controlled by one organisation or on an individual basis. Often they are subject to a tender process. In order to maximise "profit" "prime" positions are often sought - usually in areas where there is the maximum number of people, be near entrance/exit gates, front of stage. Such positions can cause obstruction, leading to overcrowding, blocked access routes and consequently are dangerous. Careful consideration must be given to siting such units away from access routes (a minimum of 6m from gates) and in less dense areas of the crowd, ie outside the site lines. Some units will have highly flammable products such as LPG and must be sited accordingly.

Circulation space and potential queuing arrangements should be considered.

s) perimeter fencing

Whether or not a perimeter fence is required depends upon the type and nature of the event/crowd and consequently a risk assessment approach. Such fences may be necessary to prevent trespassers entering the site and for the safe management (capacity) of the crowd.

Some events may not require a fence at all, or merely a stake and tape/steward barrier whereas others may need a sophisticated substantial fence or multiple arrangement. The crowd loading on such structures and the climbing potentials should be assessed. Such fencing should be able to cope with large numbers of people pressing on it and should be able to withstand a crowd loading of at least 2kn/m tested at an appropriate height usually between 1.1 and 1.5 metres. It is recommended that they should be approximately 3 meters in height, difficult to climb and be free from dangerous projections. A typical arrangement for large concerts is an opaque inner fence with an outer "see through" fence - providing a moat in which security can patrol. To minimise the climbing of the inner fence for those who have breached the outer, a 5m gap is usual to prevent the run up approach. Sometimes, three fences may be used to facilitate an emergency vehicle route. Careful consideration should be given to ground conditions, obstructions, support legs and exit and entrance requirements.

t) front of stage barrier requirements and arrangements

A front of stage barrier may be required particularly if significant crowd pressure is expected. A risk assessment of the event having regard to the evaluation of the artiste and audience profile, together with the capacity should assist in determining whether or not one is required and if so what type and design is required. For most large concerts some form of front of stage barriers will be necessary.

Depending on the final outcome of the assessment, various front of stage barrier configurations are possible:

- single demarcation barrier non-crowd loading.
- single crowd rated systems.
- double or triple barrier arrangements forming penned areas.

If a venue has restricted space, a straight barrier is suitable. However, for large concerts, particularly those outdoors, a convex barrier extending into the audience may be preferable. It should form a curve across the main performance area, extending to the ends of the side stages. It should be erected in conjunction with escape right and left.

If using a multiple barrier arrangement escape and capacity arrangements must be carefully considered and controlled. (See chapter 12 (a) Barriers)

u) signage

The location and size of all signage is critical when designing a site. For indoor/permanent venues signage normally has a place for items such as fire exits, extinguishers points, entrances, car parks, emergency vehicles points etc and will meet the appropriate British Standards. For supplementary facilities and all outdoor green field site this will not be the case.

The effective use of signs provides a rapid way of conveying orientation in your site design, direction and emergency information. It thus assists in crowd flow. Signage should be:

- clearly visible
- understood

From a site design perspective the size and position is very important. Large outdoor venues will require signage of a larger type than British Standard in order that it can be seen from a distance. Fixture points may well have to be provided and accommodated for.

v) welfare facilities

The number and type of welfare facilities, ie sanitary accommodation, water supply and information will depend upon the type of event, but once numbers have been agreed these need to be located within the design. Sanitary accommodation should be distributed around the site in a manner which does not block site lines and serves its greatest need, eg near bars/catering concessions. If non-main units are to be used access for the employing tanker should be planned. They should be clearly visible and well signed. Queuing areas should not obstruct any gate emergency route etc.

Water supply is normally situated next to sanitary accommodation. If tankers are used the space requirement and ground drainage will need to be considered.

Information points vary from a notice board to a mini marquee. The size and location must be taken into consideration. It should not be located near to any gate or emergency access route since people using or hanging around the facility could cause an obstruction. (See chapter 9 (g) Welfare Services)

w) excess visitors

The subject of excess visitors to an event is normally the consequence of free and non-advance ticket shows. However, such measures may necessitate the design of a holding/queuing area. Such facility may be substantial in size, accommodating exit gates and welfare provisions and consequently need to be accommodated within the design.

x) final site design

Once all the necessary details/requirements have been finalised each should be drawn to scale on a site plan having regard to spacing requirements etc. The final plan should then be reassessed to check the occupant capacity (having regard to site lines and circulation space) emergency/crew/public access and egress. Power distribution and generation positions can now be finalised. It is inevitable that changes will be made up until site build. It is important that each change is evaluated.

Richard Limb of The Symonds Groups has written this section on Event Safety Management and his advice is very much appreciated. You can find his contact details in the listings at the back of this book.

> "But it is pretty to see what money will do"
>
> *Samuel Pepys 1633–1703*

chapter eleven

sponsorship

a) definitions

"An agreement to give money to a charity on the completion of a specified activity by another."

(Oxford Dictionary)

"Payment of money by a business to an organisation for the purpose of promoting its name, products or services. Part of the general promotional expenditure of a business, and can encompass a sense of corporate or social responsibility."

(Arts & Business)

"A mutually beneficial business arrangement between sponsors and sponsored to achieve defined objectives."

(D.C. Watt)

There are some golden rules well worth following for those seeking sponsorship. A professional approach to obtaining sponsorship will aid, but never guarantee success. There have been occasions in the past when individuals have almost stumbled upon sponsorship support but it becomes less likely every day as businesses become more hard-nosed about the returns they can expect from any sponsorship package. They will have clear ideas about what they want and they will assess any sponsorship proposal on its ability to deliver to their requirements.

Finding sponsorship can be very hard work and event organisers should recognise this, allocating time or specific individuals to undertake this work as for other tasks within the organisational structure.

Sponsorship is about building a mutually beneficial business relationship with another organisation. It is important that everybody recognises that:

- there are benefits to both parties and these should be agreed at the start
- the defined (hopefully shared) objectives of each party should be identified and understood by each other
- sponsorship must have something in it for everyone

There has to be a close match of stated objectives if the sponsorship arrangement is going to be sustained and successful.

Identifying an appropriate sponsor is difficult enough, but then persuading them to get involved is the most difficult aspect. Reaching the right person in the company means that you have to spend time researching the organisation. They may possibly use an agency for all of their sponsorship deals, or may have a headquarters which is not based locally. You may get passed from department to department, then ultimately to the protective Personal Assistant who is the fire-wall protecting the Chief Executive.

Because it is so difficult to reach the decision-maker, you will also need to have a long lead-in time. Usually budgets run from April to March and in order to be included in a company's sponsorship plan, you will need to approach them well in advance of the start of their budgeting exercise. An approach in November for example with a well-packaged proposal may not reap rewards until 18 months time.

Honesty is the best policy when you are trying to attract a sponsor. Don't make promises you can't keep; don't exaggerate what the benefits might be and don't raise expectations which can't be delivered. You are possibly trying to build a long-term relationship and having respect for your sponsor will bring rewards.

b) the meeting

Having identified your ideal sponsor and having made sure that your product has some synergy with their objectives, make an appointment for a first meeting. Your approach now needs to be very professional. This is a face-to-face opportunity to 'sell' your product. You will, of course, have researched the company as far as you possibly can using, for example, Companies House and the Internet, etc. The package you will be offering is tailor-made to suit their company aspirations and strategies.

Keep the first meeting brief by presenting your event concept and without going into too much detail. You can present a potted history of previous events where sponsorship has worked well, using some relevant examples which may interest your new potential sponsors. Provide information about who your target audience is and the type of activities you are planning to stage. Have a minimum sponsorship sum in mind but do not discuss this at the first meeting. You need to give your sponsor time to think and to fully digest the information you have prepared.

Identify event components

1 identify exactly what constitutes the event
2 break the event into appropriate parts to clearly specify what is on offer to a potential sponsor
3 these parts should be made available to potential sponsors individually, in a group or in total

Specify sponsorship opportunities and benefits

1 list exactly what is on offer for any potential sponsor
2 specify the value attached to each part of the whole package available
3 display a positive benefit package
4 look at the package from a sponsor's point of view – is it designed to meet their needs?
5 leave enough flexibility in the package to dovetail with the sponsors needs

Clarify roles and responsibilities

1 state exactly what the organising agency will do for the sponsor e.g. in terms of media relations or corporate hospitality
2 clarify exactly who will do each of the roles required
3 suggest how the overall sponsorship package will be delivered

If you are seeking an exclusive sponsor, you will need a fully comprehensive package with the maximum benefit clearly established for the company. If you are seeking a number of sponsors for specific aspects of an event, you will need to make a list of opportunities available, starting with the most important.

Before the meeting ends, you need to find out:

- whether the person you are meeting is the ultimate decision-maker
- if they would like you to present a fully-costed proposal - based on your discussions
- what the "ballpark" sponsorship figure might be
- the next meeting date and a note of who will be there when you present the proposal

c) sponsorship proposal

When compiling your proposal, you need to think about the needs of your sponsor:

- what are their corporate priorities?
- who are they trying to reach?
- what kind of exposure can they expect to receive (from the press, television, etc)?
- are there branding opportunities?
- will they be highly visible at the event?
- can you arrange for them to meet other 'decision-makers'?
- will there be point-of-sale/display/exhibition opportunities?
- are you prepared to collect data on their behalf?
- is this an exclusive sponsorship arrangement or do they have to share the event with other sponsors?
- could they have merchandising rights?
- will they be able to present awards/trophies, etc at the event or mark their presence in some other way? Many sponsorship proposals fail because the searcher fails to put themselves in the shoes of the company being approached.

Your proposal needs to be professionally compiled. It should contain:

- event title, date and place
- contact name of the organiser (or sponsorship officer)
- duration of the event
- the theme
- event objectives
- dynamic colour images demonstrating the image and branding to be used (especially on publicity material)
- photographs
- breakdown of expected audience
- outline marketing plan
- list of benefits to the sponsor
- other potential partners
- testimonials from previous sponsors.

Make the proposal informative, with clearly stated objectives, but with sufficient flexibility to make it attractive. Make it short, easy to read and to the point. Busy Directors or Chief Executives do not have time to read long documents – prepare just a few pages (2 or 3 maximum).

At the next meeting you can add to your proposal verbally:

- tell them that they will be invited to join your events planning team and give them some ownership of the event

- answer any questions
- if you have approached other companies, be honest about it.
- be flexible – adapt your proposal according to what you hear at the meeting

If you feel that you are receiving the right signals ask if the event is of interest to them, assess and agree how much it is worth to them and close the deal.

d) a written agreement

A written agreement for the sponsorship arrangement is essential for all concerned. While it need not be a lengthy legal document for smaller events, include at least the following items:

- the identity of the parties involved
- the particular role that each party is contracting to undertake
- a definition of the rights and benefits for each party
- a definition of exclusivity of rights or benefits
- identification of who is responsible for the delivery of these rights and benefits
- how and when payment is to be made
- the protection of ownership of names, logos, emblems, etc relating to the event
- royalties, broadcasting rights, merchandising rights
- provision for the termination of the sponsorship arrangement as a result of default on either side
- provision for event cancellation
- provision for alterations in the sponsorship agreement if the value of the event changes dramatically, eg television coverage is either added or withdrawn

e) potential problem areas

Like so many things, sponsorship is great if it works but ranges from difficult to disastrous if it doesn't. Beware of potential problems and keep on top of them:

They include:

- mismatching: arising out of the difference between the sponsor and the sponsored over conflicting aims, ambitions, targets or views.
- misunderstanding: this often arises from the lack of a clear explanation of what both parties want and what they hope to get out of the arrangement
- deceiving: this can be due to a sponsorship-seeking agency not accurately representing what they can actually deliver and try to 'con' the sponsor

- non-delivery of benefits: related to what can practically be delivered - being unrealistic can eventually result in the non-delivery of previously promised services
- withdrawing of sponsors funds: it is possible that due to changing business circumstances that a sponsor may withdraw their support with or without good reason. This is one reason why a written agreement is absolutely vital
- change of image: if something happens to change the image from positive to negative then the sponsor may be upset and wish to withdraw from a potentially negative association
- cancellation: cancellation of an event can be damaging for all concerned and major sponsorship should not be sought or taken for an event which is liable to cancellation, without a clear understanding of this possibility by all parties
- misadventure: if something negative takes place during the event, e.g an accident, injury or violence, it can cause major embarrassment for everyone and potentially damage sponsorship relations
- specialist advice: both parties may wish to take outside advice before becoming involved in a sponsorship agreement, especially if they are inexperienced in this area
- insurance: each party should consider covering themselves for cancellation risk, major catastrophies or other losses from their side of the deal.

f) do's & don'ts

A list of do's and don'ts in seeking and working with sponsors:

do
- have a clear idea of your target audience
- create a fully-costed marketing plan
- spend some time on creating an attractive package
- make your "product" flexible
- set out your unique selling points
- get your sponsors on board in the early planning stages, invite them onto the team
- keep sponsors involved all the way through the planning stages, during the event as well as the planning for future years
- clarify with your sponsors what they want from you in return for their support
- build long term relationships with sponsors
- make sure you know the rules about VAT on sponsorship monies
- treat sponsors as VIPs at the event they are sponsoring

don't

- leave short lead-in times
- specify initially the amount of money you are looking for – ask what the 'package' might be worth to them
- make promises you can't keep
- "take the money and run"

in short

- remember to thank your sponsor at the end of the event
- be professional, be honest, be fair and have respect for your sponsors. You may want them again in the future.
- provide a written report on the event including some qualitative and quantative information

The crucial steps to remember in looking for sponsorship

- think like a business
- analyse the vehicle you're offering
- set SMART objectives
- fit into the promotional mix
- choose a partner with care
- plan carefully
- build trust and co-operation
- set aside a complementary marketing budget
- monitor and evaluate
- do it even better next time!

g) VAT on sponsorship and donations

Sponsorship is the general term used for financial or other support, such as the giving of goods or services by businesses to sport, the arts, the educational sector and other businesses.

If something is supplied to a sponsor in return for the sponsorship then a taxable supply is made. It does not matter how the sponsorship is described; what counts is the terms under which it is provided. If the sponsorship is provided on condition that clearly identifiable benefits are supplied in return (such as publicising the sponsor's business or products or making facilities available to the sponsor) then VAT must be added to everything received under the sponsorship agreement.

The publicity may be, for example:

- an event, concert or display named after the sponsor
- the sponsor's name being incorporated in the name of a team or of a team's horses, or displayed on a team's vehicles or shirts.

If, on the other hand, nothing is done or given in return for the sponsor's support - a pure donation - a taxable supply is not made and the sponsorship can be treated as outside the scope of VAT.

However, to be treated in this way, the sponsor's support must be entirely voluntary and must secure nothing whatever in return. If the only acknowledgment of the sponsor's support is a simple mention in a programme or annual report and nothing else is required, it will still be exempt.

However, if a contribution is made on condition that the sponsor's name or trading style is advertised or promoted, or that the sponsor receives some sort of benefit (such as 'free' tickets, beneficial booking rights or 'free' advertising), then it is considered to be a taxable supply and VAT must be charged.

If a sponsor gives a donation in addition to providing sponsorship under an exchange agreement, the donation can be excluded from the amount on which VAT is added provided that:

It is clear that the donation is entirely separate from the sponsorship; and

The amount of sponsorship is realistic in relation to the benefits provided to the sponsor

Clearly, if benefits are provided to the sponsor on condition that the sponsor gives the donation, it is part of the consideration for the supply and must be included in the amount on which VAT is charged.

Donation of goods

True donations of services or money are outside the scope of VAT. Gifts (donations) of goods from registered donors must be accounted for by the donor on the cost of the gift (unless the cost is £15 or less). If the gift is used for the purposes of the business, VAT can be reclaimed as input tax subject to the normal conditions.

Newspaper and magazine competitions

Publishers of newspapers or magazines who run competitions for which prizes are donated may have a general understanding that the donor will benefit from some publicity as a result. However, provided there is no specific contractual obligation to provide advertising or publicity in return, there is no supply of advertising to the donor and therefore no need to charge VAT. The donor would treat the supply of the prize(s) as a business gift. But if there is a clear contract under which the donor provides the prize on condition that advertising is provided, a taxable supply is made to the donor and again, you must account for VAT. Furthermore, if the donor is registered for VAT, he or she must account for VAT on the open market value of the prize(s).

Value for VAT purposes

VAT must normally be accounted for on everything received under a sponsorship agreement, including anything which is distributed as prizes, paid over as expenses or secures benefits for the sponsor. Where goods or services are received from the sponsor in return for services under the terms of the sponsorship agreement, this is a form of barter and there are two separate supplies. The sponsor must account for VAT on the value of the goods or services supplied and the recipient of the sponsorship must account for VAT on the open market value of the services supplied to the sponsor. This will normally be equivalent to the value of the goods or services received from the sponsor.

Where the agreement provides that the amount of money to be paid by the sponsor depends, for example, on the success of the sponsorship, VAT must be accounted for on the actual amount received.

VAT registered sponsors must be issued with a tax invoice for the amount of which VAT is accounted. The sponsor can then reclaim the VAT as input tax, subject to the normal rules. If the amount agreed makes no reference to VAT it must be treated as VAT inclusive, unless a separate charge for VAT is made.

Sponsorship for non-business activities

Sponsorship for something which is not by way of business may be treated as outside the scope of VAT unless supplied on such a scale that it constitutes a business in its own right.

Agents

The VAT treatment of sponsorship is the same whether or not either party employs as agent. An agent must account for VAT on any commission received.

Overseas sponsorship

Supplies involving advertising and publicity rights to overseas sponsors may quality for zero-rating. If you enter into any 'unusual' sponsorship agreement not clearly covered by the above, you are advised to consult your VAT office.

Public authorities

Goods and services supplied to government departments, local authorities, embassies, foreign missions and international organisations in the UK are taxable in the usual way and tax invoices must be issued.

Certain goods and services, supplied by government departments and local authorities will be taxable and tax invoices will be issued in the usual way.

Croner's Reference Book for VAT provides excellent financial advice on sponsorship and thanks are extended to Croner's for agreeing to the section of VAT on sponsorship being reproduced. Further details on Croner's Reference Book for VAT can be found at the back of this book.

h) sources of information for sponsorship

- internet
- Yellow Pages
- newspapers
- business rates register
- business organisations
- professionals
- participants
- library
- market research
- past partners
- existing sponsors

i) support

Sponsors might support an event for the following reasons:

- community awareness
- public awareness
- low-cost promotion
- media interest
- publicity
- competitive advantage
- association
- promotional campaign
- customer/client entertainment
- event exposure
- commercial benefit
- image
- public good
- donation
- target audience
- corporate relations
- reflected glory
- marketing tool
- personal interest
- philanthropy

j) some useful sponsorship websites:

- Leisure Training Consortium
  www.leisuretraining.com
- Institute of Sports Sponsorship
  www.sports-sponsorship.co.uk
- BDS
  www.sponsorship.co.uk
- The Sports Sponsorship Advisory Service
  www.sponsorship-advice.org
- European Sponsorship Consultants Association
  www.sponsorship.org

chapter twelve
infrastructure

Having undertaken your site inspection (see Chapter 9c), and carefully considered the rules of procurement (see Chapter 6), it is now time to consider what will be required on site in terms of convenience, comfort, welfare and the health and safety of all participants.

The following information needs to be considered within the context of all the site features, facilities and amenities.

a) barriers

Definitions:

Barrier: Anything that bars passage or prevents access.

Factors:

- preventing access or passage
- demarcation of designated areas
- forming unauthorised areas
- level of security
- density or movement of people
- controlling the level of attendance at an event
- creating safe zones
- vehicle movement

On a site plan of the event, all designated areas will need to be clearly marked. The above factors will need to be considered in deciding if a barrier system is required and more importantly what type of barrier is needed (please also refer to the section on fencing).

Barrier Systems *(Physical or Passive)*:

- ground markings
- coloured tape
- security personnel
- vehicle crash barrier
- vehicle rise and fall bar
- mesh fronted pedestrian barriers
- crowd (anti-surge/crush and front of stage) barriers

See section on fencing

- mesh-fronted fence panels
- solid light-duty fence panel or hoarding
- solid heavy-duty fence or hoarding

Stability:

Each particular barrier will have limits to the amount of horizontal force it can take before it becomes unstable.

Whether the force is applied by people, the wind or a combination of the two, the chosen classification of use needs to be carefully married up with the correct barrier type. For example you would not install a lightweight barrier in a crowd, crush or anti-surge situation.

Health and Safety:

Site or event risk assessments and emergency plans should help in the correct identification of, or the putting in place of, the right barrier in the right place. If you are unsure, then seek advice.

b) fencing

The need for fencing within or around an event will be driven by factors such as those listed below.

Glastonbury

Factors:

- preventing access or passage
- demarcation of designated areas
- formation of unauthorised areas
- level of security
- line of sight or visibility

A site plan of the event should be drawn up, which indicates all proposed fence lines and the reason for the requirement of a fencing system. The information shown on the plan should help in the selection and procurement of the correct fence system.

Fence Systems:

There are a variety of fence systems to choose from such as solid braced fence panels ranging from 2.5 to 3.0 metres in height, open mesh fences, which can range from one to two metres in height and lightweight hoarding panels. If perimeter security is a high priority then specialised fence systems can be employed which can range from 4.0 metres plus, with optional overhangs to deter climbing. Typical materials for fence systems are aluminium, steel, plastic coated steel, galvanised steel and plastics.

Stability:

Whether a fence is one metre or four metres high, great care has to be taken with regards to the stability of the fence. The higher the fence system then the greater the potential for a fence failure. It is important to obtain or agree with a local authority the wind speeds that a fence system must withstand. A competent person or the supplier of the fence system will give you the designed wind speed reaction or capabilities.

Crowd forces also play a major part in the stability of a fence. There are standards that quantify crowd forces a fence system must withstand, again a competent person or the fence suppliers will advise. A professional installation is the final criteria for a successful fence system.

Health and Safety:

As mentioned above, fence stability is a factor that has major health and safety implications. It is important to know the fence limitations or design limits. Once these have been discovered the associated Site Plan Risk Assessment should have action points, evacuation and possible dismantling procedures if the wind conditions start to encroach on the design limits. Always ensure that a perimeter fence has the correct access and egress facilities for emergency vehicles and to meet the emergency evacuation criteria.

Do not leave it to chance; an emergency plan is essential.

Diversification:

If noise and environmental sound contamination is a problem for the surrounding residential area or the local authority stipulates sound contamination reduction, the use of solid fence systems can be adopted as acoustic barriers.

c) temporary access bridges (pedestrian and vehicle)

There are situations where a bridge is the answer to overcome access problems for vehicle traffic or pedestrian movement. At some events pedestrian bridges are used to keep the public safe and to minimise traffic disruption outside the event area,

Wimbledon

which can provide non-interrupted pedestrian access over a busy roadway. Vehicle bridges are often used to bridge small streams or rivers or to bridge large ditches or trenches. The aim of the bridge is to keep pedestrian and traffic flows moving over obstacles in a safe manner or environment.

It is essential that all bridges are erected safely and therefore you must ensure that competent contractors are employed and that all bridges used have an appropriate design certificate.

Factors:

*   gross and axle weights of vehicles that may be using the bridge

Festival of the Sea

- temporary footings or foundations
- ground bearing capabilities
- informing the local authority if a temporary bridge passes over a road or highway
- check if planning permission is required from the relevant local authority
- suitability of the bridge in emergency procedures
- bridge conforms to Bridge Codes and the relevant British Standard relating to the material used in the construction of the bridge
- stability during high winds
- check if it is possible to hang advertisements or banners from the bridge
- typical Temporary Bridge Systems
- show typical pictures of bridges and materials used

Health and Safety:

The issues in relation to health and safety focus on the competence of the company to provide, construct and certificate a temporary structure such as a bridge. Documentation is important, along with appropriate hand-over certificates. All plant used in the fabricating and erecting of the bridge must have In Scope Inspection and Test Certificates and all plant operatives must have the relevant proof of training or plant licence. You may need to seek advice or

Chelsea

Goodwood

employ a health and safety specialist or engineer to work on your behalf.

d) pedestrian walkways and coverings

A pedestrian walkway or ground covering system is the means of allowing pedestrians to walk safely and securely around an event or arena without restricting the flow of people from one position to another.

The walkway may have more than just one function (ie conveying people from A to B). It may need to carry lightweight traffic movements or be installed as a ground protection system. The factors that need to be considered when helping to choose the correct pedestrian walkway system are listed below.

Factors:

- grass or ground protection
- the need to run vehicles on the walkway or cover
- the duration for which the walkway will be installed

- gradients and existing ground conditions
- performance in the wet (skid resistance values)
- aesthetics of the walkway
- wheelchair access or compliance
- predicted density of pedestrian traffic

Health and Safety:

The pedestrian walkway must have the minimum skid resistance value in wet and dry conditions and comply with walkways in public places. The installation of the walkway or cover must be done without leaving any trip hazards (i.e. walkway tiles are placed without leaving up-turned corners or level differences between tiles). If vehicles intend to use the pedestrian walkway, then check the limitations and maximum vehicle weight.

e) temporary access roads

Temporary access roads are primarily used to give vehicles a sound, firm platform, and to prevent them becoming stuck on soft ground. The temporary access road also possesses properties to evenly distribute loads in areas where applied ground pressure must be minimised, such as, driving over underground services or basements. Some of the factors that will help you decide if a temporary access road is required are listed below.

Factors:

- preventing vehicles from becoming stuck in soft ground
- to protect the ground from rutting
- to give motorists clear roadways to follow

Goodwood

Goodwood

- to lower applied ground pressures, especially for heavy vehicles such as cranes and lorries
- to provide temporary car parking facilities

The temporary access road panel can also be used for other load distributing applications including crane lifting platforms with high outrigger loads and for load distributing pads for stanchions from stages sitting on soft ground.

Some design considerations when utilising temporary access roads include:

- gradients and cross falls
- vehicle speeds and traffic calming measures
- turning circles (especially for large vehicles)
- localised troughs in the ground
- inspection chambers
- underground services.
- pedestrian crossing points
- very soft ground (roadway may need to be double thickness)

Health and Safety:

Under the health and safety banner it is important to understand that the event organiser ensures that sub-contractors and suppliers are competent and any equipment that they use on site conforms to current health and safety legislation. Check that crane operators have an up to-date plant licence and that the equipment they use has the necessary inspection and test certificates. Is there a site-specific risk assessment? You may need to seek advice or employ a health and safety specialist to work on your behalf.

This section on barriers, fencing, walkways and coverings, temporary access roads and temporary access bridges has been generously supplied by Eve Trakway. Their details are listed at the end of this book

f) toilets

Whatever happens, try to avoid the 'queuing for the loos' scenario. There is existing guidance from the Guide to Health, Safety and Welfare at Pop Concerts which sets out guidelines for sanitary accommodation provision.

Organisers should ensure that adequate sanitary conveniences are provided for the number of people expected and that consideration is given to their location, access, construction and signage. They should not be situated in the vicinity of food stands.

To minimise crowding and queuing problems, sanitary conveniences should, where possible, be located at different points around the venue rather than concentrated in a small area. In deciding on the location, the need for access for servicing and emptying should be taken into account. Portable no-mains toilets are fine for long term use providing that they are serviced properly.

Numbers of conveniences required will depend on the type of event, clearly one where heavy alcohol consumption or camping is to take place will demand a higher number of conveniences. These figures assume a 50:50 male/female split.

Female conveniences: 1 WC for 100 females

Male conveniences: 1 WC for 100 or fewer males
2 WCs for 101-500 males
3 WCs for 501-1000 males

The above figures assume an event duration of eight hours. They may be reduced in the following way for shorter concerts:

Duration of concert	Percentage of above standard
More than 8 hours	100%
6 hours	80%
4 hours	75%

It is recommended that a wash hand basin should be provided per WC.

Please note that these are guidelines only.

g) banners

There is an increasing need for the external PVC promotional banner when it is correctly manufactured, sized, coloured, 'graphicked' and sited. This can be a very cost effective method of advertising when all things are considered, but how much do we know or need to know when purchasing one or more of these versatile message carriers?

There are two main types of PVC material: supported and non-supported. This has nothing to do with the way they are hung, but relates to whether the PVC has a material substrate or not. If there is, then it is referred to by its weight - grams per square metre (gsm). If there is not it is referred to by its micron thickness i.e. 350 microns.

Strength is the relevant factor in tear resistance. Supported is stronger than non-supported and the heavier the better. For one-day shows and throwaway banners you can use an economy grade - say, 400 gsm.

For banners that require longer use or that will be subjected to windy conditions you will need a heavier grade - say, 550 gsm. The proper use for non-supported PVC is internal and where they do not come under any strain. Ensure that banner makers use the correct type of PVC for the job in hand.

Some materials are often not suitable because the PVC was not specifically formulated for banner use, so you could find that screen printing or vinyl lettering will not adhere to the surface satisfactorily.

The manufacture of banners is carried out in two ways. One is with welded seams and the other is with stitching. Both ways are effective, but stitching leaves a flatter hem which perhaps looks better.

How do you hang your banner? Eyelets are the favourite method, which allows you to pass rope through the holes or cable ties, thus supporting your banner.

Bridge on a golf course

The eyelet should have raised teeth so that when compressed into the banner the teeth grip the material substrate, helping to prevent the eyelet being pulled out under strain. Pole pockets is another method and the size of the sleeve in the banner is dependent on the size of the pole.

Rope can be sewn into the seam which is useful if the banner is to be strung high up or between buildings. If used across a road then wire rope should be utilised for safety's sake.

If you want your banner seen from both sides, then you need a special banner material called Total Block. This has a light blocker built into the material so that you do not get ghosting from the message on the other side. Colour is something to consider. Most people have standard white, but why? Professional banner makers hold a stock of standard colours which, when used correctly, can add much power to the impact of your messages. In fact, dual background colour, i.e. one half yellow and the other black, or other combinations, is being pioneered to great success.

What to put on your banner? Text can be signwritten or more usually, vinyled to ensure excellent results as it will adhere to the flexible surface and weather the elements and will also endure the physical rolling and unrolling of the banner on many occasions to no ill effect.

The thing to remember is impact. A short, sharp, punchy slogan in a large and clear typeface that can be seen from a distance is bound to be better than a fussy, illegible and overcrowded message.

If you are considering 10 or more banners with the same message, then screenprinting is usually the more cost-effective route to take. Whatever method you use you must ensure that the banner is going to be properly and efficiently put into place. Poor hanging gives the banner a bad reputation.

The banner must be taut and then it will display its message and your company's image to the most effect. One of the best ways is on a specially manufactured banner frame.

Taking care of your banner is easy. If it has vinyl applied then make sure the banner is rolled back onto a tube with the graphics on the outside. This helps the vinyl not to pucker. But above all, make sure the banner is put away dry, otherwise it could deteriorate.

If you want more advice or help concerning banners then contact Boldscan Banners and Frames. Their contact details appear at the back of this book.

h) signage

One of the most important factors in organising your event is to ensure that your visitors find your venue with ease. How do you go about ensuring your road signs are in the right places and will stay there? There are two options:

Option 1

Arrange and complete the task yourself. You need to do the following:

- complete a survey of the area and decide what routes your visitors will use
- taking into account the local authority's policy towards temporary road signs, draw up a schedule of locations for road signs
- the schedule must specify the exact fixing point including the number of the lamp column, the size of the sign and the layout
- make sure that your schedule complies with all legal requirements for road sign design and fixing
- approach the local authority with a detailed planning application and ask for their permission to erect the signs
- indemnify the local authority against any incident arising from your signs
- arrange public liability insurance for signs with cover for at least £5million for any single incident
- liaise with the local authority to ensure that, where possible, permission is granted with enough time for you to have the signs made, negotiating legal points where necessary
- once permission is granted, make the signs to legal standards of reflectivity, lettering size, colour and design
- within an agreed timeframe, erect the signs in the approved locations, ensuring that they are securely and safely mounted without damaging the post and fixed to laid down requirements of height and distance from the road edge
- while erecting signs ensure that you are complying with Safety at Street Works Act for work on the highway
- while signs are in position, be able to return to each location to remedy any problems arising that are notified by the police and/or local authority
- within 48 hours of the event finishing, return to the signs and remove them, once again complying with the Safety at Street Works Act for working on the highway
- store or destroy the signs

Option 2

The Automobile Association will undertake all of this work for you. An 'average event' (if there is such a thing) involves the use of about fifteen signs. The AA will examine the requirements of each event and will charge a price which reflects the work involved.

The AA Signs department is not a profit-making concern but is a service which covers operating costs only. Thanks are due to the AA for providing the information on signage. Contact details for the AA are listed in the back of this book.

i) marquees and tents

Marquee and tent hirers have a duty to ensure that members of the public can have complete confidence in the safety of the marquees and tents that they erect. In turn, organisers need to ensure that their suppliers operate to a code of practice when supplying marquees and textile-covered frame structures.

In addition, ancillary equipment supplied for use with structures such as flooring, lighting, furniture, interior linings and heating should also be erected and installed in accordance with an approved Code of Practice. Usually such structures are supplied on a short-term or temporary basis. Long-term hire (i.e. more than 28 days) or semi-permanent installations, may be subject to other codes or regulations outside the scope of a limited period of a Code of Practice.

The Made-Up Textiles Association (MUTA) represents users, processors and manufacturers of all kinds of industrial textiles and is active in promoting technical standards in the industry. MUTA has published a Code of Practice for fabric structures and organisers are advised to contact MUTA for advice when considering the erection of temporary marquees and associated services.

In a bid to achieve even higher standards of public safety, a national training qualification for marquee erectors has been established.

This is the first time that a formal training qualification for operatives in the marquee hire industry has been set up. The initiative has come from the MUTA which represents more than three quarters of the UK's marquee hire industry.

It is estimated that around 5,000 workers are involved in the business of erecting and finishing marquees, hospitality villages and sports events marquees throughout the UK.

j) road closures

Event organisers need to consider not just those involved in their event but also everyone affected by it. Many events (of any size) will affect traffic flow and planning must be considered carefully with this in mind.

Detailed discussions with the police emergency services and other relevant agencies and community groups will be essential to ensure everything is taken into account and all essential permissions are obtained. Failure to follow mandatory procedures is a step to disaster and can cause last minute panic and ultimately cancellation.

It is all too easy to see this as a minor straightforward matter but unless it is properly handled it can be problematic. Like so many items in event planning, it requires serious detailed thought and appropriate action.

Normally any significant traffic interruption (over thirty minutes) will require an application form and a formal road closure. This is not something that can be left to chance or arranged at the last minute. It will usually take a minimum of eight weeks to arrange. Remember – check it out. Speak to the police and the local authority officials at the start of your planning stages.

k) policing

Event organisers should remember that probably their best friends are the local police, provided that you behave appropriately and involve them from the beginning.

Police attitude is very positive and generally supportive if you get them involved and keep them informed so that they can do their job as successfully as possible.

For the police force and indeed any stewards helping them, the key must be that they are there to help, not just control. They have a key role in genuine customer care, not customer discipline.

The key word used throughout should be involvement. Police should be represented on organising groups and be seen as an integral part of the planning and delivery of any event from start to finish.

They will have specific rules (and good behaviour) to enforce during the event and that is healthy and necessary. Good relationships can help get the best mutual approach to the policing of any event.

Give the police as much notice as possible that your event is happening because they will need to let you know exactly how much they will be charging for your event and costs could increase if you give them a very short lead-in time. On the other hand, you may already have a good working relationship with the local police force and can persuade them to either waive or reduce their charges.

> "Nothing is more dangerous than an idea, when you have only one idea"
>
> *Alain 1868–1951*

chapter thirteen
other event components

a) catering

Nearly all events involve catering services to some degree. How should an organiser start planning the provision of catering services? Catering is probably one of the most important aspects of any event. If the food and drink is good, the event is a success (so say the participants!).

The first consideration is that of identifying needs. To do that the organiser needs a clear idea of the nature of the event that they are organising. The factors affecting need to include:

* how many people might attend?
* what is the duration of their visit likely to be and how far might they have travelled prior to arriving?
* how close is the event to existing catering outlets?
* does the programme for the event include specific breaks for refreshments?
* are there special needs to provide catering for sponsors, sponsors' guests, VIPs, staff, volunteers and performers?
* is catering included in the admission price?

Satisfying needs is a minimum requirement

The assembly of people at an event also offers a range of commercial opportunities which might be exploited. Some events will require the event organisers to benefit financially to a substantial degree from the catering. Other types of events will provide an income from catering to the organisers - but it is the caterers who stand to benefit most financially from exploiting the opportunities available.

Such is the range of catering requirements at an event that you may need the services of a local voluntary group such as the Women's Institute, a one-person operator with a hot-dog van or the specialist events division of the largest catering companies in the country.

There is a clear distinction between seeking caterers to provide opportunistic catering services such as hot dog stalls, beer tents and ice cream at an event and seeking a caterer to cater for your specific requirements such as meals for conference delegates/sponsors' guests, free hospitality bars, etc.

The difference is primarily that in the first case 'the event caterers' are selling their produce to the people at the event and taking the financial risk, therefore they must decide whether there will be sufficient trade for them to cover their costs and make a profit.

In the second case, which we will call 'the outside caterer', the caterer is selling services that you have pre-ordered. They know in advance the service, standards and quantities that are required and the price that has been agreed for these services.

At an event such as the Royal Horticultural Association Chelsea Flower Show all these catering components are present.

'The Event Caterer'

Consider the following points:

* of the people attending, how much might they spend on catering products and what type of products are they likely to purchase? Are people likely to bring their own refreshments?
* during the event, will the people attending be free to purchase catering services at any time or only at certain times?
* over what period must the service be provided? What are the get-in and get-out times?
* how extensive will the competition from other catering services be? Are exclusive concessions available for particular products or services? Are there opportunities for combining the provision of a service with sponsorship of the event? What licenses or regulations will be required?
* what utility services are available and what site constraints exist?
* how much equipment is going to be required to prepare, produce and serve catering products and, therefore, what is the financial risk to the caterer?
* what happened last year?

The opportunity dimension of the catering at an event is something that caterers themselves will be able to judge provided they have good information about the event. The organiser will need to be able to summarise that information on a fact sheet at an early stage. It is an essential tool in making approaches to caterers where the organiser seeks to profit from attracting caterers to an event. That process will vary according to the type of event and could consist of:

- Advertising the catering rights for all aspects of the event in return for a fee. The organiser will detail not only particulars of the event but will also need to specify the minimum services to be provided. It is important not to over-specify as this might reduce the financial return to the organiser. Bids will have to be compared, references may need to be taken up and checks made with Environmental Health Officers. A presentation may also be requested before deciding on the best bid, i.e. the one that confirms a good price with an expectation of an appropriate quality of service. Only the largest events, often involving more than one day, are suitable for this process. A formal contract is required. The contract may be renewable for future years. Terms of payment will be specified. If a variable basis based on an element of income share is used, then it must be possible for the organiser to check on the amount due (see chapter 6 on purchasing).

- Offering concessions at the event for particular products, eg hot dogs or ice cream. The organiser needs to take care to ensure that if a concession is offered, that it is enforced at an early stage. The agreement needs only be a simple one. The cost of the concession needs to be specified and the payment arrangements (preferably in advance or on the day) made clear. The arrangement may for example be per ice cream outlet, leaving the caterer free to decide how many outlets need to be brought onto the site. Bids could be invited for concessions. Some voluntary bodies may want to offer their services.

- Remember that for outdoor community events it may be necessary to install coolers, fridges, microwaves etc. which will require power and water supplies.

Here is a typical catering checklist for an outdoor sports event:

Special guests – sponsors, VIPs, civic guests
- Private refreshment facilities with a service appropriate to the time of day and duration of attendance.
- Attended service to serve food and drinks and clear, on an ongoing basis throughout the event.
- Check: any presence required of sponsors' refreshment products? If 'yes', will this attract any special charges from the caterer, e.g. corkage, or require the caterer to provide special equipment, e.g. champagne glasses.

Officials, first-aiders, stewards, staff, contractors
- conveniently situated refreshment services with a service appropriate to the time of day and duration of attendance.

- identify items that are free, e.g. tea and sandwiches. Items that are available to purchase, e.g. wrapped confectionary; items that are not to be supplied, e.g. alcoholic drinks.
- may need to be associated with rest area and people may need space to eat on their own.
- refreshment tickets/identification needed.
- special needs, eg cold drinks in hot conditions.

Competitors
- similar to above.
- some events may include team teas, event dinners or similar. Entry fees may be inclusive of refreshments, eg childrens drinks and snacks.
- special check: eating and drinking times relative to participation in event, special requirements such as drinks during an event.

Spectators
- range of sales points appropriate to the time of day and duration of attendance.
- special check: licensing regulation, possible rules of event restricting services, eg no alcohol or no glasses. Are there times in the programme when catering services will be in peak demand?

'The outside caterer'
When an outside caterer for your event is required, some careful research is needed to ensure that you appoint the appropriate type of caterer for your requirements.

Where to start looking for caterers:
- directories and internet listings
- trade association lists, e.g. MOCA (see section on MOCA at the end of this section)
- Yellow Pages and similar publications such as Caterer and Corporate Entertainment
- recommendation

Carry out a check on the companies which you identify.
For instance, undertake a telephone 'audit' to find out if the catering company answers the telephone promptly, puts the call through to someone who can answer all of your questions and offers to have a meeting to discuss all your requirements. The manner in which they deal with your enquiry will give you a good idea of their customer/client care policy.

In order to brief your caterers adequately, consider the following points and questions:

- how many covers can they cope with?
- state the time of day or night the event takes place

- provide details of the venue. Is there a kitchen available for preparation of food or will portable kitchens need to be brought in? Do they need to hire tables and chairs?
- are you clear about get-in and get-out times?
- let them know what your exact budget is and ask what kind of meal you can expect for your money.
- who provides the menus?
- make sure that they are aware of any special guests and whether special arrangements need to be made for them, e.g. if the meal is a buffet, you may not wish to have your guests standing in a queue and would need a reserved table with waiter/waitress service.
- state the composition of the group of special guests.
- can they adequately cater for special dietary requirements at short notice?
- it should be ascertained as far in advance as possible whether the guests have any special dietary requirements. However, if this information is not available at the time of ordering your meal, make an allowance of 25% of the total covers to be vegetarian food and 5% for vegans. Other more specialised requirements should also be discussed as soon as these are known.
- will table gifts be provided? If so, to whom?
- it is essential that you determine the type of cutlery and crockery to be used. Costs are dramatically reduced for disposable plates, cups and cutlery but this seriously detracts from the quality of the meal.
- the style of service should be determined in advance. What is required?
  - silver service
  - waiter/waitress services
  - buffet - stand up
  - buffet - seated
  - buffet - finger

Remember to prepare the copy for your invitations well in advance, remembering to include the date, time, place and dress code.

The event will run far more smoothly if stewards are on site to direct guests to the correct room or reception in advance of the meal.

The following is a checklist of items which you may wish to consider when compiling your catering plan:

- [ ] after-dinner speakers
- [ ] toastmaster
- [ ] top table protocol
- [ ] call to dinner
- [ ] pre-dinner receptions
- [ ] pre-dinner drinks
- [ ] cloakrooms
- [ ] caterers: ask for examples of similar events references - also from any sub-contractors
- [ ] staff resources
- [ ] own equipment
- [ ] responsibility for missing or broken items
- [ ] insurance
- [ ] financial arrangements
- [ ] floral decorations
- [ ] colour themes
- [ ] menus
- [ ] venue (marquee, etc)
- [ ] greeting and seating
- [ ] car parking
- [ ] performers/entertainers
- [ ] physical requirements
- [ ] rehearsal time
- [ ] master of ceremonies
- [ ] refreshments
- [ ] arrival times
- [ ] sound checks
- [ ] technical requirements
- [ ] contact day before
- [ ] welcome on arrival
- [ ] check if all arrangements are on time fifteen minutes before meal is ready to be served
- [ ] payment

Appreciation is recorded to Mike Fulford of Leisure Advice for contributing to the section on catering. His contact details can be found at the back of this book.

The Mobile and Outside Caterers Association (GB) Ltd (MOCA)

Mobile and outside catering is generally accepted as a High Risk Activity, usually due to the large number of people provided for.

For several years MOCA has been striving to improve standards within the industry with the introduction of a Due Diligence System and MOCA Safe Food Level 1 and 2 Training Courses.

The Association continues to work closely with Environmental Health Departments and other national bodies and is committed to promote and improve food and general safety within the industry.

MOCA aims to provide general guidance and basic standards for caterers operating from mobile trailers, marquees and market stalls in addition to those providing sandwich and buffet services and portable/mobile bars.

The general principle can be applied to both caterers and those wishing to employ the services of catering companies in almost any situation, from a roadside sandwich bar to a show/event caterer and a mobile buffet service working from fixed kitchen premises.

The Code is a voluntarily accepted document and is based on 'good practice' but where there are legal requirements it will be clearly stated.

MOCA recognises and accepts the need for positive attitudes to health, safety and hygiene throughout its membership and the industry in general. In doing so it will take all necessary steps to assist and encourage members to manage their food businesses to the highest possible standard.

In order to achieve the objective of its policy statement, the Association will:

- co-operate fully with all enforcement authorities to achieve high-quality food safety management
- encourage and facilitate suitable training of all food handlers to appropriate levels of skill and knowledge
- encourage and assist members to work closely with the relevant enforcement authorities to secure for themselves a safe food business.

There are differing levels of membership. Members wishing to join to a level other than the basic entry membership undertake annually a diagnostic survey of their food handling arrangements known as their 'Annual Declaration', in addition to agreeing to random inspections and the use of the MOCA Due Diligence system. Guidance appropriate to the needs of the membership is given to ensure that good hygiene and safety practices are employed where food is prepared, handled, stored, transported and sold.

In particular, members will be routinely required to:

- in all ways comply with all current legislation
- identify and appropriately monitor all temperature controlled appliances and take immediate remedial action in the event of operational failure
- ensure that all surfaces are restored to their original state of cleanliness as soon as practicable after use
- maintain an orderly system of stock rotation, ensuring that all food in storage is used in its proper turn and does not become misplaced
- take all reasonable precautions to ensure that food is not exposed to risk of contamination either by their behaviour or lack of cleanliness
- ensure that good order and tidy conditions are maintained and that extraneous items, unconnected with the food business, are not allowed to accumulate in the preparation area
- keep the amount of food in storage to a workable minimum, ensuring that quantity and need are kept in balance
- identify and eliminate all entry routes and harbourage area for pests and attend to any relevant structural deficiencies
- rectify any damage or disrepair to the structure of the unit, facilities or equipment associated with the safe handling of food
- ensure that gas and electrical systems are safe and in good working order, and regularly checked by a competent person.

The following questions need to be asked:

- how does the event organiser ensure that they have both the best and the safest caterers?
- what precautions should the organiser take when employing caterers?

Again, 'Due Diligence' applies to both caterers and event organisers. The consequences can be serious if such diligence is not properly applied.

Many organisers have not yet realised that the concession fee could be the least of their worries if things go wrong. Following a recent settlement of £1million for a pregnant mother who contracted salmonella from a salad, organisers need to take a serious look at what they are doing and why. It is not simply a matter of checking the caterer's insurance policy. If the caterer is not acting within the law, it is possible that the insurer could legitimately 'walk away' from any claim. That would leave both the organiser and the landowner fairly and squarely responsible as it is unlikely that, without insurance, the caterer would be able to meet a substantial claim.

The answer is that the organiser needs to carry out his/her part of the 'Due Diligence' trail by checking more than the caterer's insurance certificate. This need not be a burdensome task as most items that need checking can be done at the time of tendering or contracting the caterer. It is suggested that organisers should ask questions - and get copies of relevant documents - and ask questions such as:

- is at least one member of staff per unit trained to Basic Food Hygiene level?
- do you operate a due diligence system? If so, which one?
- include a copy of your last gas compliance certificate / electrical compliance test certificate
- what source of power do you use?
- if you use petrol, what size petrol tank do you have?
- how much LPG do you carry?
- what refrigeration and freezing capability is there on your mobile(s)?
- are your staff uniformed? Do they wear hat and other appropriate clothing?
- what back-up storage facilities do you have?

If these and other checks are carried out, the risk of disasters would be reduced and the likelihood of liability would be minimised. MOCA advises organisers to issue a written contract with conditions clearly spelt out rather than depending on verbal agreements which, when things go wrong, can end in angry exchanges and lost reputations.

It is advisable for any event organiser to check that any outside caterers they use are members of MOCA, so ensuring that best practice is implemented as outlined above. Thanks are due to MOCA for providing information for this section. See back of the book for further details.

b) ticketing

Admission by 'ticket only' is the ideal way of effectively managing the number of people attending an event, but a decision about pricing levels is always difficult.

If an event is being staged for the first time, with no history of past success or failure, organisers may need to charge low ticket prices in order to buy customer loyalty for next time. Pricing also depends on the target audience, and whether there are other competing events in the same area.

If tickets are to be sold, the box office service is key to encouraging customers to attend year on year. Make it easy for people to buy tickets. The sales effort at the box office (or lack of it) can make or break the relationship with the organiser's potential audience.

For example, if organisers install a telephone hotline booking

service, make sure calls are answered promptly and that the answering service is available at the publicised times. Make sure the customer is charged the correct amount, particularly if there is a concessionary ticket regime, or differing pricing levels are in operation.

Also make sure that everyone is always clear, staff and customers alike, about who is entitled to receive concessionary rates. Publicise the policy for unsold tickets. Can people turn up on the day and buy a ticket? Will tickets NOT be available on the day? Are there stand-by arrangements?

Kalamazoo Security Print Limited issue a warning about ticket forgeries: 'Whilst the actual cost of ticket fraud is uncertain - partly due to a lack of knowledge of how many tickets are forged and also due to an unwillingness by organisations faced with fraud to reveal the costs - fraud is increasing in the UK. According to the Metropolitan Fraud Office, the losses associated with paper-based fraud account for more than all burglaries, robberies and shoplifting put together.

"The leisure industry in particular is constantly at risk from fraud. By forging tickets for concerts, theatres and events, criminals can guarantee a rather attractive income at the expense of the organisers, the promoters, the artists and the public.

"Tickets are particularly susceptible to fraud because of both their high face value and because of limited supply. Unfortunately, as the technology behind colour photocopying, computers and desk top printing advances, fraud becomes easier and the risk to organisations becomes greater.

"However, many organisations, both large and small, may not realise the consequences of fraud. Not only does it result in lost revenue - for the organiser, the promoter and the artist - but can also be a serious safety risk.

"Take a music concert for instance. Whether staged in a huge concert hall or small club, if tickets are copied and pass off for sale as being originals , the venue loses out on sales to potential customers. This could be simply a few pounds for a small local theatre or music event or thousands of pounds for huge, high profile, pop concerts. Whatever the specific amount, it's usually significant enough for any organisation to feel the losses.

"More importantly, by counterfeiting tickets and issuing them for sale, there are more tickets available than planned by the organisation and possibly more than the venue can legally accommodate, raising a health and safety issue.

"All entertainment venues have a limit to the number of people they can accommodate (whether seated or standing) under the Local Government Miscellaneous Provisions Act. These numbers are calculated by the Fire Authority in conjunction with the Police prior to issuing a venue with an entertainments licence. Should that number be exceeded, the organisation will be in breach of the conditions of licence and the result can be a fine, loss of licence or imprisonment. In addition, should anyone from the public be hurt through the organisation's negligence, it would also be liable to prosecution under civil law. This, of course, is a worst case scenario but one that could very easily befall any organisation that does not take care to secure its tickets against fraud.

"Many organisations may not be aware of the existence of security tickets or their benefits. Security tickets simply include special covert (disguised) and overt (obvious to the holder) features that enable the box office or ticket collectors to ensure they are authentic."

Examples of some security features include:

- unique watermarks
- ultra violet dull papers
- instant Verification paper (when the ticket is marked with an instant verification pen, it turns pink
- copy Void background (if tickets are colour photocopied, the word 'VOID' becomes visible on the forgery)
- microtext (tiny printed codes which can only be read using a magnifying glass)
- solvent-sensitive paper (ensures no alterations can be made to the ticket through the use of solvents)

Tickets can be specially designed for the customer and incorporate any number of security features or the customer can choose to overprint customised information onto standard security tickets.

Remember that the licensing authority will require an audited account of the number of tickets sold. It is essential that tickets are numbered in order to lay the audit trail. Collection of tickets at the entrance to a venue is also very important and will help to avoid illegal entry.

Kalamazoo Security Print Limited have contributed the technical information to this section on Ticketing and their advice is very much appreciated by the authors. You can find their contact details in the listings at the back of this book.

The following is a list of tactics you may wish to implement when selling tickets for your event:

- provide a ticket hotline
- all return slips on brochures should be tagged in order to identify the most effect sales methods
- any advertisements in newspapers should carry a ticket booking slip (tagged) and should also carry a hotline number with a credit card booking facility and also a method of payment through Giro (post office)

- publicity material must state who is eligible for concessionary tickets
- sell tickets at outlets other than the theatre, eg civic centre, library and other most frequent places in the area
- brochures should list stockists and sales points
- notices can be placed in post offices advertising discounted ticket rates for senior citizens
- brochures should contain information about catering facilities, content of the event's programmes and venue access times
- contact social secretaries of groups/clubs offering party bookings (warning: group discounts may need to be restricted to certain performances)
- provide an 'easy to book' system
- install a booking office at the venue or on site to be open during the week prior to the event and to be open every day
- brief box office staff to 'close sales' (ie persuade the uncertain customer that they should buy a ticket)
- use an advertising feature, eg 'ticket prices remain the same as last year'
- offer multiple attendance discount or season tickets
- if the event is a festival, set up a subscription scheme for 'Friends of the Festival' to encourage audiences to commit to purchasing tickets early
- insert brochures into newspapers
- try money-off coupons/gift vouchers
- 'standby' tickets could be heavily discounted and made available just hours before the event to attract marginal customers; advertise this only a couple of days prior to the event
- consider selling 'preview' tickets to show/concert dress rehearsals at discounted rates to lower income groups
- consider providing free car parking – if this is possible, use it as a promotional feature
- research rail travel/show packages if trying to attract audiences outside the area
- consider whether the event should coincide with or avoid school holidays

c) badges and passes

Image, branding and security are being increasingly important at events and there is a demand for better ways of badging as a security measure.

One of the key changes in the way badges look is the fact that there are so many security features available these days, partly due to an increase in demand for better security. These features can range from fully personalised passes with a photographic or holographic image, as well as specialist security printing. Software is now available which is designed to allow or prevent access to events through a pre-programmed barcode reader. In addition, reports on attendance figures can also be produced by downloading the data captured from the barcode reader onto a standard PC.

The way that badges and passes are worn has also changed dramatically in recent years. Attaching a badge/pass no longer needs to be a tedious task and need not harm clothing and organisers are always looking for ways in making wearing a badge more fashionable. Printed lanyards have become an increasingly popular method of attaching badges and passes, not only because they are comfortable as they sit around the neck, but also because they open doors to sponsorship opportunities and are increasingly being used as another way of promoting corporate image.

Printed lanyards can be produced through a variety of methods, ranging from dye-sublimation for superior quality, woven or the more budget-friendly screen printed process. Lanyards are also available in a range of widths and attachments, including dog clips, swivel clips and crocodile clips.

Badges or passes can be housed and attached in many ways, catering for all budgets and sizes. Flexible wallets, which are available in a wide range of colours to match corporate image are ideal for large events, whereas professional rigid card holders are more suitable for high profile events/launch parties/VIP hospitality.

Printed yoyos are also increasingly used at events. Yoyos are a fun way of attaching passes and, like lanyards, a company logo can be printed onto the yoyo to enhance corporate identity.

Badges are available in a variety of formats depending on the requirements for any particular event. They can be as simple or as detailed as required. For events where security and personalisation is less important, badges are available just with non-variable text such as the event logo or VIP. However, for events where security is of high importance, badges can be fully personalised with a person's name, photograph and their company. They may also include more specific access rights such as certain days that a person is allowed access to the event.

The use of Ultra Violet paper as a security feature on event badges is very effective. However, it can only be used on paper-based badges and there is an increase in the use of PVC/all plastic badges now in the events industry, especially at more prestigious events where security is paramount. The Ultra Violet option is also one of the most expensive, making it less desirable to organisers.

Barcodes are still one of the most popular methods as, with

the aid of a barcode reader pen at the event entrances, participants can easily be identified and denied or given access to the event, especially if a photograph is used in conjunction. Also, with barcodes various data and reports can be produced after the event on who gained access and who didn't show, etc.

Other key security features that are being increasingly used to prevent badge forgery are:

- <u>Holographic images</u> – used on PVC badges and laminated paper passes. They are a simple and cost-effective method whereby a small 'difficult to copy' image is placed on the badge in a visible position. This prevents reproduction through photocopying or scanning

- <u>Security overlay</u> – a clear film that is over-laminated onto the badge (usually PVC badges) and contains repeated "security" text or logo. It also offers extra protection against wear and tear, combined with a 2D image that refracts under normal lighting

- <u>Security print</u> – rather than having a plain background on the badge, a security print is often used. It incorporates a wavey fine line design (often with UV links)

- <u>Photo-sensitive paper</u> – this is a type of paper where after a certain time, writing appears on the paper, such as "VOID" or "EXPIRED". This is good for events that last several days where people may only be allowed access to one of the days.

- <u>Vestigial imaging</u> – a replication and repeating of the badge holder's photo – ghosted into the background.

This information was provided by Anthony Tidy, Marketing Co-ordinator at Identilam plc. Full contact details are available at the back of this book.

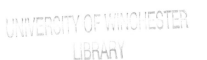

d) firework displays

If you are organising your first display, you will find these notes very valuable. If you have had experience of organising previous displays, please use them as a checklist.

i) choosing a venue

Always choose your venue in daylight. Make sure that it is large enough to accommodate your firing area and the number of spectators expected. Ensure that you can achieve the minimum safety distances required. Bear in mind that the number of spectators tend to increase each year.

Consider how you will deal with disabled spectators.

Ensure that the site has plenty of unobstructed access and exit points. You will need at least one vehicle access point for emergency vehicles.

Ensure that noise from the display will not cause distress or disturbance to nearby hospitals, rest homes, animal sanctuaries or farm animals.

It is a great advantage for the site to be well served by public transport, thereby reducing the need for car parking facilities.

To some extent the choice of venue will determine what kind of fireworks you buy. If your site is level (eg a sports field) you would be well advised to use a large number of aerial fireworks (so the spectators at the back can see). If your firing area is elevated, ground level fireworks can be used to good effect.

ii) the firing site

Remember that the spectators should be placed with their backs to the prevailing wind so that any smoke or debris blows away from the crowd. Be prepared for a sudden change of wind direction and have a reserve firing area available.

The area should be away from overhanging trees or overhead wires and cleared of any combustible materials, including long grass and undergrowth.

The area should be securely fenced off before setting up the display, ideally with interlocking crowd barriers or chestnut paling. If you use rope and pin, use two lines of rope or tape, one at the top and another half way down.

Spectators should view from the front of the display only and not from the sides or back.

iii) who should be informed

The police need to know of any large gathering of people and any possible traffic congestion.

The fire brigade and ambulance service. They need to be notified of the display and the emergency vehicle access point to the site.

The local authority. Discuss your display with the local authority officer who will advise you on your duties under the Health and Safety at Work Act as well as noise nuisance. It is also worth checking whether they know of any other displays on the same night which may compete with your own.

The coastguard. If the site is near the sea, this will avoid possible confusion with distress flares.

The airport. Inform air traffic control if the site is near an airport.

Hospitals, old people's homes, animal sanctuaries and farmers. All should be notified.

Give everyone the VENUE, DATE and TIME.

IT IS STRONGLY RECOMMENDED THAT YOU HOLD AT LEAST ONE MEETING ON SITE WITH THE POLICE, LOCAL AUTHORITY, FIRE BRIGADE, FIRST AID SERVICE AND AMBULANCE SERVICE.

If you are organising a small, private display, you should still notify the police and anyone who may be disturbed by the noise.

iv) stewards

Provide as many as you can and ensure that they are easily identified. Fluorescent waistcoats are ideal. The recommended minimum number of stewards is two for the first fifty spectators and one for each additional 250. Brief the stewards beforehand on the site layout, the plans for the evening and how to evacuate the site in the event of an emergency.

v) first aid services

Should be invited to attend and be on duty half an hour before the crowds arrive and remain until the site is clear.

vi) firing team

This is covered in more detail under 'Firing Procedures' below but as a general rule the number of personnel should be kept to a minimum.

vii) entrances and exits

Ensure that there are sufficient numbers of entrances and exits for spectators to be admitted in an orderly manner. Do not allow spectators to bring their own fireworks onto the site. Publicise that fact well in advance.

viii) public address

For larger displays a public address system should be provided. Hand-held loud hailers are very useful for smaller displays.

ix) bonfires

If you are having a bonfire ensure that it is well away and downwind from the firing area. It should be fenced off and supervised before, throughout and after the display. Do not use flammable liquids to light the bonfire and exclude anything hazardous from the bonfire material, e.g. aerosols, tins of paint, bottles etc. if there is any risk of hot debris from the bonfire landing in the firework area DO NOT LIGHT THE BONFIRE. Make sure that the bonfire is completely extinguished before leaving the site.

x) firing procedures

The number of operators should be kept to a minimum and preferably should have some experience. Each operator should have a particular firing job allocated and should familiarise him or herself beforehand.

Study the firing instructions and fireworks well in advance, preferably a day or two before the display.

All fireworks with aerial effects should be angled away from spectators so debris falls where it cannot cause injury or damage.

NEVER ANGLE FIREWORKS OVER THE HEADS OF SPECTATORS.

xi) portfires

These are specially designed for lighting fireworks and are supplied. Only use portfires to light your fireworks. Do not carry portfires in your pockets. Leave them in a convenient place on the firing site in a closed box.

xii) fire fighting

An adequate number of fire extinguishers and supplies of sand and water should be provided. Certain stewards should be trained in the operation of fire fighting equipment as advised by the local fire brigade.

xiii) first aid

Have on the firing site a first aid kit. Include in the kit a roll of kitchen cling film and clean water. Clean any wound with water and wrap in cling film (excluding any parts of the face). Cling film is sterile, does not stick to wounds and protects burns, cuts and grazes until medical treatment is available.

xiv) personal equipment for operators

Make sure that every operator is equipped with the following:

- overalls - cotton, preferably non-flammable (never use nylon)
- safety helmet
- eye and ear protection
- gloves
- torch
- hammer and nails
- scissors
- pliers
- bailing wire or strong hemp cord
- matches

We strongly recommend that you check the Fireworks Regulations 2004 (ISBN 011049542X), website: www.dti.gov.uk/ccp/topics1/fireworks.htm.

The authors are grateful to Pains Fireworks for this section on firework displays. See back of book for address.

> "Two wrongs don't make a right, but they make a good excuse"
>
> *Thomas Szasz 1920–*

chapter fourteen

legal aspects

a) Legal differences in the UK

Whenever dealing with events legislation, it is vital to remember that we are operating in the United Kingdom; each of the constituent countries (and sometimes local authorities) can have different laws and regulations. It is always worth checking with local lawyers and experts. The variances (eg in licensing laws) can be significant and have a major impact on events.

In particular, the differences between English and Scottish law are large and to treat them as the same would be a big mistake. Historically, and right through to the present day, legislation on a whole variety of civil and criminal matters have quite different legal implications. Failure to adhere to the appropriate legislation could render the event organiser liable to prosecution.

This chapter is only a simple guide and neither the author nor the publishers can be held responsible for its total accuracy or for any errors.

b) Health and Safety at Work Act

The Health and Safety at Work Act (HASAWA) is an umbrella act which covers a great number of regulations, most of which apply to all companies and services that make up our industry. These regulations include:

- the Noise at Work Regulations
- the Health and Safety (First Aid) Regulations
- the Reporting of Injuries, Diseases and Dangerous Occurrences Regulations (RIDDOR)
- the Electricity at Work Regulations
- the Control of Substances Hazardous to Health Regulations (COSHH)
- the Lifting Plant and Equipment Regulations
- the Workplace (Health, Safety and Welfare Regulations)
- the Management of Health and Safety Regulations
- the Health and Safety (Consultation with Employees) Regulations 1996

- personal Protective Equipment Regulations
- provision and Use of Work Equipment Regulations
- the Manual Handling Operations Regulations
- the Display Screen Equipment Regulations
- the Health and Safety (Signs and Signals) Regulations
- the Firework (Safety) Regulations

The Health and Safety Executive can provide you with free leaflets, books (priced) and other easy-to-follow guidance on all of the above regulations and related subjects.

c) licensing

i) phonographic performance ltd (PPL)

PPL is a music industry collecting society which collects licence fees from broadcast and public performance users on behalf of record companies. This licence fee revenue, after deducting running costs, is distributed to PPL's record company members and performers.

PPL grants licences for the use of sound recordings in the UK to all broadcasters, which includes the BBC (television and radio), independent television broadcasters and production companies, commercial radio, and cable and satellite channels.

In the public performance sector, the PPL licenses the whole range of users which includes clubs, pubs, hotels, restaurants and shops as well as individuals such as exercise instructors and dance teachers.

People do not always understand that the possession of records, tapes or CDs does not give the automatic right to broadcast or play them in public. Copyright law protects recorded music and this makes it possible for musicians and record makers to receive payment for their work when it is played.

Who needs a licence?

Anyone playing recorded music in public. Examples include discotheques, pubs, clubs, hotels, restaurants, shops, leisure centres and dance and fitness instructors.

'Playing in public' usually means anywhere outside the family circle and also applies to members-only clubs.

Licence fees vary according to usage and there are tariffs to cover the whole range of uses. Where appropriate, these tariffs are negotiated with the relevant national organisations representing the different music users.

Playing PPL members' records in public without a licence is an infringement of copyright. It is also illegal to copy sound records and PPL has to pursue anyone found to be making copies of recordings for a subsequent public performance. Penalties for copyright infringement include High Court injunctions to prevent further use of records, or the award of damages, which can be expensive.

Contact details for the PPL are listed in the back of this book.

ii) the Performing Rights Society (PRS)

The PRS (the Performing Rights Society) is an entirely different organisation to PPL. The PRS is a membership organisation which collects licence fees for the public performance and broadcast of musical works. It distributes this money to its members – writers and publishers of music.

A PRS licence allows you to use all types of music from all over the world - legally. Whether the music is live or played on a tape or CD player, jukebox, radio, video, TV or karaoke and whether or not the performers are paid - a PRS licence is a legal requirement.

PRS Public Performance licences are required by premises which use music. These range from concert halls and dance halls through public houses, hotels and restaurants to ships, aircraft, hairdressers, doctors and dentists waiting rooms and even telephone 'holding' systems. A PRS licence is usually reassessed annually and is referred to as a 'blanket' licence.

The law states that if you wish to use copyright music in public, you must first get permission from every single writer or composer whose music you intend to use. And 'in public' means broadly anywhere outside your domestic circle. However, it is obvious that making such individual arrangements for licences would be virtually impossible, thus the PRS deals with this for you.

PRS will work out the charge for your particular premises using the appropriate tariff for your business and will explain the charges to you.

Contact details for the PRS are listed in the back of this book.

iii) Public Entertainment Licence (PEL)

You are required to obtain a PEL licence when staging any entertainment involving live performers, including karaoke and discos (people dancing at a disco or singing at a karaoke are regarded as performers).

PEL licences are granted subject to inspection by the issuing Local Authority after they are satisfied that the premises meets environmental and safety standards. The cost of a licence will depend on the maximum capacity of the premises and the opening hours and can be issued on an annual or occasional basis.

There are variations in the application procedure in different parts of the country. In the first instance you should contact the appropriate London Borough Council if you are inside London or the appropriate District Council if you are outside London.

Various examples of where a PEL is required are available on the website. Just type into the search engine the words 'Public Entertainment Licence'.

d) contracts with agents

It is important to understand that when you contact an entertainment agency on the telephone and agree to book an artiste, that this is a binding verbal agreement which would stand up in a court of law.

Each agency will have their own performance conditions as every artiste performs for different timeslots, ie some 30 minutes, some 40 minutes, etc. Make sure that you see a copy of their performance conditions before signing a contract. It is usual for performers' food, accommodation, travelling expenses and so on to be included in the contract so make sure that this is the case.

You will need to fully brief the Agent regarding the type of audience you expect to attend, i.e. gender, age range, numbers. You will also need to provide full information regarding the venue at which the performance will take place, i.e. indoor/outdoor, purpose built theatre, green field site with full stage facilities, sports centre, etc. Some entertainers will not perform in sports centres, or outdoors and it is essential that the Agent is fully aware of the type of venue which is being considered. The agent must know what power supply is available, ie single-phase, three-phase; whether there are special dressing rooms available and access times to the venue.

Expenditure can be greatly reduced if a purpose-built venue is to be used, with proper dressing rooms, catering facilities and sound and lighting systems. If the venue is not purpose built, or is a temporary structure, where portacabins or marquees are to be used, it can be extremely expensive to create the infrastructure for the event, particularly when the 'star' of the show demands their own dressing room, toilet and catering facilities.

A standard contract outlines all the terms and conditions and it can be expensive to have it checked by a Solicitor, so make sure that the solicitor is experienced at working within the entertainments/music industry.

The following clauses taken from a typical contract show the thought processes you may need to go through when scrutinising contracts:

Clause:

The Artiste reserves the right, if they have chart success before or on the contracted play date, to renegotiate the fee.

Your response may be:

Addition to clause: ... to renegotiate the fee providing that no tickets have been sold for the performance on (date of event).

(Organiser - please note: Tickets sold to customers who wish to see a particular performer form a contract between the organiser and the customer, and the non-appearance of the expected performer will result in a breach of that contract).

Clause:

All financial settlement to take place with (artiste) by (date).

Response:

It is typical that you have to pay in advance, especially for a famous act as agencies frequently ask for a 50% deposit. If the event does not take place the artiste will expect the agent to pay their full fee.

Clause:

Venue to provide a selection of sandwiches, mineral water, soft drinks and beers.

Response:

Ask the agent to be prescriptive about quantities and frequency of catering. If there is a large number of performers, such as an orchestra, with a rehearsal and performance spanning a whole day or more, the volume of catering could significantly increase the organiser's costs.

Some Agents do not include any clause relating to cancellation by an Artiste. Those that do, undertake to supply another performer 'of a similar calibre'. Frequently it is impossible to replace the contracted Artiste of the same calibre (i.e. Robbie Williams, Billy Connolly, Phil Collins, etc) with a performer who would satisfy the customer, who has contracted with the organiser to see that particular artiste.

It is advisable to discuss this point with the agent at the outset of your negotiations and to ensure that the organiser has insurance cover in place for cancellation by artistes or for any other reason resulting in cancellation of the event.

The Complete Talent Agency (CTA) has provided advice and information for this section on contracting with Agents. More information about CTA is listed at the back of this book.

e) byelaws

It is impossible to be too specific about byelaws as they are by their very nature local. For every event organiser, however, one thing is certain – there will be a number of byelaws which potentially affect any event.

They concern many issues including:

* street trading
* opening hours
* licensing
* drinking in public places
* dog fouling
* litter
* public performance
* road closures

It is essential that you check with your local council to see which ones affect you – there will be some! It is also worth checking with your local police force.

Please remember that byelaws change from time to time, so it is always advisable for event organisers to keep the situation under review in case new byelaws are introduced during the planning stages.

Such byelaws can be quite quirky and in the UK there are several legal and political systems in operation. For example, Scots law and English law can be quite different and allowances must be made for this.

f) The Children Act 1989

Even if your events are not organised specifically for children, they may attend your event, perhaps accompanied by an adult and you must take account of the requirements of The Children Act 1989.

Consider the health and safety of children attending your event and include them in your risk assessments. Ensure you provide appropriate services and facilities and that these are managed by organisers with appropriate experience and expertise (remember that you must carry out appropriate checks of individuals dealing with children).

Consult the Guide to Health and Safety ...... Chapter 22 for further guidelines and advice. Also see the Welfare Section f), Chapter Nine in this book.

Essentially – familiarise yourself with requirements of The Children Act 1989.

g) Disability Discrimination Act 1995

The Disability Discrimination Act (DDA) aims to end the discrimination which many disabled people face. This Act gives disabled people rights in the areas of:

- employment
- access to goods, facilities and services
- buying or renting land or property

Final rights of access came into force in October 2004.

i) who are disabled people?

People of all ages, backgrounds, beliefs and life stories have disabilities. There is a common misconception that disability equates to wheelchair use. In fact, only 5% of disabled people are totally reliant on a wheelchair and a further 5-10% use them only when they go out. Over 1 million people have visual impairments and more than 8 million have hearing impairments. Probably the most neglected group in terms of site provision is the million people with learning disabilities.

ii) maximising accessibility

Accessibility is a comprehensive issue that is rarely resolved by single-focus prescriptive actions. Instead, it requires a broad-based approach that considers together issues such as physical site layout, off-site and on-site information and interpretation, education programmes, quality of visitor experience and opportunities for involvement and site use.

It is an essential requirement for organisers to be aware of the implications of the Disability Discrimination Act on their event and more information can be obtained from the Disability Rights Commission – www.disability.gov.uk

> "What we call the beginning is often the end. And to make an end is to make a beginning. The end is where we start from"
>
> *T.S. Eliot 1888–1965*

chapter fifteen

evaluation

To evaluate is:

- to determine value
- to appraise
- to find a numerical expression
- to judge
- to rank
- to assess

During the planning stages, during the build-up, at the event and during breakdown, the aim is to please everyone: the customers; the contractors; the concessionaires; staff and, of course, to meet your own standards.

So how was it? Was it a successful event? If so, is this just personal perception? What did everyone think? It is important to gather information to find out what people really think.

At the planning stages, by setting clear objectives, they form success criteria. Use an appropriate variety and quantity of relevant information to measure event performance and establish suitable mechanisms to compare event performance with the objectives set. The correct level of commercial confidentiality should be maintained, where financial returns are crucial.

Qualitative data will provide valuable information which can be used to improve future planning, performance and delivery.

Ask if the event met all of the objectives set? If not, why not?

Everyone involved in delivering and attending the event should be included in the evaluation process. They all have something to contribute, they have all acquired experience that can contribute to continually improving good practice. All staff, paid and voluntary, should also be consulted. Evaluation should involve monitoring and should be continuous and ongoing, ie prior to the event; during the event; and after the event.

Each component of your event should be evaluated and in this chapter you will find an example questionnaire aimed at trade, voluntary and charity exhibitors at a local authority-run show.

a) monitoring and evaluation

Evaluation can be measured in terms of:

- Feedback
- Comparison
- Recognition
- Finance
- Cost Effectiveness
- Quality
- Staff Morale
- Attendance
- Activity Levels
- Standards of Performance
- Customer Satisfaction
- Use of Resources
- Achievement
- Deadlines
- Relationship
- Social Inclusion
- Equity
- Participation Levels
- Frequency
- Aims
- Objectives
- Success

Finally, for evaluation purposes it should be remembered that in the leisure business although it is sometimes all about bottom line profit, it can also be about building community capacity or other softer outcomes.

We may well want to try to evaluate -

Tangible/Quantifiable	Intangible/Qualitative
Objectives met	Community involvement
Statistical returns	Sustainability
Attendance levels	Image
Profit/Loss	Volunteer Input
Success Criteria	Future Commitment

There is also a risk with events of just measuring the inputs against the outputs whereas the long term impact can be significant.

b) example of an exhibitor survey at a summer show

Could you please take a few moments to complete this survey. Your comments are very valuable and will assist with the organisation of next year's show. *Thank you.*

1	How did you hear about the show? (*Please tick as appropriate*)					
	newspapers	leaflets	poster displays	word of mouth	radio	direct mail
	attended before	other (*please specify*)				

2	Have you exhibited at the show before?	Yes		No	
	If yes, how many times?				

3	Do you feel that the show provides you with good value for money?	Yes		No	

4	Was your overall impression of the event:			
	Very good	Good	Satisfactory	Poor
	Comments			

5	How valuable do you think the show was in making people aware of your services/products?		
	Very valuable	Valuable	Not valuable
	Comments		

6 | How do you rate the quality of the organisation of the show and of the amenities on site?

	Very good	Good	Satisfactory	Poor
Pre-show administration				
Information pack (manual)				
Help on the day				
Access to the site				
Show layout				
Toilets				
Water				
Information point				
Entertainment				
Comments				

7	Will you be exhibiting at next year's show?	Yes	No

8	The show is financially subsidised by the Council in the same way as swimming pools and libraries, to the value of several thousand pounds. Do you think it is important for the Council to continue to support the show in this way?	Yes	No

9 | What would be your suggestions for improving the show? (*please indicate on the reverse if required*)

10	Would you like to receive further information about the Council's events	Yes	No

Name	
Organisation	
Address	

Thank you for taking the time to complete this questionnaire. The survey will be collected by a member of the organising team on Sunday afternoon. Alternatively, please return by post to:

> "Knowledge is of two kinds. We know a subject ourselves or we know where we can find information upon it"
>
> *Samuel Johnson 1709–84*

chapter sixteen

special events information and checklists

The following checklists are compiled on the assumption that the basic programming for your event has been undertaken. They are designed to help you implement your plans.

a) conferences/seminars

- [ ] Create a critical path with timeframe (see example Critical Path on page 12)
- [ ] Prepare budget
- [ ] Book venue (see Venue Inspection Form for inside events on pages 111-115)
- [ ] Contact speakers
- [ ] caterers: ask for examples of similar events references - also from any sub-contractors
- [ ] Brief speakers on date, time, place and conference theme
- [ ] Confirm audiovisual requirements with speaker (slides, video, Microsoft PowerPoint)
- [ ] Provide visual aids preparation guidelines
- [ ] Confirm overnight accommodation
- [ ] Arrange rehearsal room for slides, etc.
- [ ] Send travel instructions, car parking arrangements, location of railway station, copy of final programme to speakers and delegates
- [ ] Notify speakers about check-in/check-out arrangements at hotel and items that you will/will not pay for
- [ ] Notify speakers about travel/expenses claims
- [ ] Ask for highlights of presentation for publicity purposes
- [ ] Request estimated time of arrival/departure
- [ ] Tell speakers name of room to be used and number of delegates attending
- [ ] Appoint audiovisual company to provide:
- [ ] Stage set (see below)
- [ ] Lecterns
- [ ] Logos for stage set
- [ ] Speakers' table
- [ ] Microphones

Identify chairperson. Provide

- [ ] Briefing notes
- [ ] Speakers' biographies to aid introduction
- [ ] Domestic announcements
- [ ] Emergency evacuation procedures to be read at the start of the day

General

- [ ] Prepare delegate information pack
- [ ] Delegate name badges
- [ ] Delegate list
- [ ] Prepare a copy of final programme with venue/room names against each session
- [ ] Compile conference delegates evaluation sheet
- [ ] Prepare lunch tickets, invitations, etc.
- [ ] Produce signs
- [ ] Produce 'reserved' signs/speakers' nameplates
- [ ] Hold on-site meeting with venue contact immediately prior to conference
- [ ] Final briefing with chair immediately prior to conference
- [ ] Ensure refreshment breaks provide soft drinks and water as well as tea and coffee
- [ ] Invoice delegates and send acknowledgement letter, travel instructions, venue information

Before you go

- [ ] Compile a conference/seminar list before leaving the office: do not rely on your memory
- [ ] Prepare a delegate questionnaire for issuing at end of event
- [ ] Leave copy of the following at the office:
  - [ ] Telephone number of where you are staying
  - [ ] Telephone number of the conference/seminar venue

- [ ] Map/travel instructions
- [ ] Delegate list

On site

- [ ] Set-up registration desk
- [ ] Erect signs
- [ ] Position speaker name-cards on top table
- [ ] Count chairs
- [ ] Check number of chairs at speakers' table
- [ ] Hold rehearsals for audiovisual presentations
- [ ] Check that you know where light switches are situated
- [ ] Check blackout arrangements are satisfactory
- [ ] Ensure venue contact has your programme timings
- [ ] Check out location of cloakroom, toilets, public telephones
- [ ] Make sure you have local taxi telephone numbers, how to get to nearest railway station
- [ ] Fire alarm systems
- [ ] Location of fire exits
- [ ] Disabled access: lifts, toilets, catering area, number of steps if no disabled lifts, availability of ramps, availability of staff to assist
- [ ] Fifteen minutes before each break check catering arrangements
- [ ] During breaks ensure that venue has replenished water/glasses etc. on top table
- [ ] Change speakers' nameplates if necessary

Wind-up

- [ ] Thank you letters to all involved
- [ ] Invoicing to be completed
- [ ] Analyse completed evaluation forms
- [ ] Replenish stationery box for next time

Evaluation (see Chapter 15)

- [ ] What went well?
- [ ] What can be improved?
- [ ] How did staff perform? Invite self-assessment

Audiovisual provision

Most audiovisual production companies will visit the venue with the client in advance of the event to ascertain the exact requirements. This is a valuable service because you will always find some extra needs to be addressed. It is worth noting which floor the presentation room is on and if there are any tight corners which will make it difficult to move large pieces of equipment.

Once in the room, identify the full blackout facilities, and that whether they are in working order, where the house lights are controlled from and, most importantly, whether there are any obstructions on the ceiling that can block the screen. One of the most common problems with older venues is chandeliers. They look wonderful but if they are situated so that they cast a shadow onto the screen, find out whether they can be raised or removed. This can be a costly problem to solve and should be addressed at the earliest possible stage. Your event will only be successful if the audience can see the visuals and hear the words!

When considering the screen size, the ceiling height must be taken into consideration. If you are using slides, you may need to have a square screen to accommodate landscape or portrait slides. As a rule of thumb the bottom of the screen should be at least 1.2m off the floor. This will allow people at the back of the room to see the whole screen without trying to peer around the heads of others. Always try to use the biggest screen possible. The larger the room, the larger the screen needs to be.

If the room is large enough, you should consider using back projection. In order to calculate whether you have sufficient space behind the screen for back projection use this formula: 2.5 x screen width + 1 metre. The advantages of back projection are that you get a clearer image and you can have more ambient light for the audience/delegates. Sound systems are also important. Never underestimate the number of loudspeakers required. It is much better to have an even level of sound through four speakers than blasting the front row of the audience through 2 speakers and hoping that people at the back of the room can also hear.

Proper microphone usage is important. No sound engineer can get clear amplification unless the presenters talk toward the microphones. Also consider the use of lapel microphones. These should not be obstructed by clothing and should be placed about 6 inches under the chin.

Question and answer microphones may be required for a larger auditorium and it is best if these are radio mics so that they can be easily passed to the person asking the question. Again, it is important that the delegate speaks into the microphone and does not gesticulate with it.

Preparation of slides and PowerPoint images must also be taken into account. Always use light text out of a dark background. This will make for a much clearer image when projected. With PowerPoint many presenters construct their own images and the presentation may look acceptable on a monitor on your desk but may not work when projected onto a large screen. For both slides and PowerPoint always use the largest typeface possible and do not place too much text onto one image. Also, do not take the text right to the edge as this may not project onto the screen.

The brightness of data-projectors is very important. This is measured in ANSI lumens and is a good and accurate guide to image brightness. A 'standard' data projector should have a minimum of 450 ANSI lumens. It is always advisable to get the brightest projector your budget can afford. Data projectors will also project video images, provided you have a video player. VHS is still one of the most common formats but does not have the resolution and clarity of Betacam SP. Betacam tapes are of a broadcast quality and will provide an excellent image over a large screen.

If you are organising an international event, be very careful about videotape formats. Videotapes from America will be recorded using a system called NTSC and from France using SECAM and the UK system is PAL. Professional VHS players are triple standard and this means that you can play video tapes from any format. However, it is always safer to check with your audiovisual company to make sure of compatibility.

Stage sets

Stage sets will always enhance an event and will provide a central focus point for the audience. Stage sets come in many shapes and sizes with the main limitation for creativity being budget. For the small event you can use simple 'off the shelf' sets and screen surrounds. This cheaper option can be made to look exceptionally good with the addition of theatre lighting.

For the larger event, it is worth considering a custom-built set. This can be designed around the conference literature and programmes, reflecting the image for the event. Using this option you can install a corporate identity and the overall effect is to portray a very professional image to your presenters and audience/delegates.

For larger conferences it may prove difficult for the audience to see the presenter at the lectern. To help with this problem many larger conferences use video relay. This involves the use of video cameras to relay the presenter onto a screen and provides all members of the audience with a good view.

Your technicians are the key to successful presentations and as such it helps if you and the technicians can build a rapport. If you have repeat events and wish to use the same audiovisual contractor, it is useful to require the same technicians who worked on your previous events. This will greatly reduce the amount of stress for the organiser, as each party is familiar with each other's method of working.

You may wish to record the event for distribution at a later date. This could be either on audiotape or video. You can also use this to generate extra income at the event by selling on to the audience/delegates as a memento of the event or a valuable reference tool.

Finally, always give your audiovisual production company as much lead time as possible so that all the equipment and crew can be booked well in advance and remember that your AV production company will need to have access at least one day prior to the event.

AVT Limited is ILAM's preferred audiovisual and stage set contractors and the authors are grateful for their advice provided above. You can find their address and contact details listed at the back of this book.

b) street parades

- ensure you have local community awareness/involvement
- have a theme for the parade
- stage a competition for the best float. Number each float
- seek police advice on car parking, 'holding areas' for all transport participating in the parade and those who are walking
- judge the competition in the 'holding area' before the parade commences
- set up a prize table in this area
- it is easier to attract a sponsor if you have commercial vehicles within the parade
- link with a charity
- apply for a Street Collection Permit from the local authority. Try to provide twelve months' notice
- if you or the charity is collecting cash, what happens to the buckets of money en route?
- consider whether you will be including music in the parade and, if so, who will provide and how many 'sets' of music will be acceptable/entertaining?
- apply for a Public Entertainments Licence if you intend to include music and dancing
- plan the route (avoiding passing the entrance of the ambulance or fire stations!)
- you may need to hire crash barriers
- consider whether portable toilets will be required
- try to ascertain from the local authority whether there are any road works due to commence immediately prior to or on the parade date
- contact local utilities companies to ensure they have no road digging operations on the parade dates
- compile a signage schedule
- is the parade insured?
- estimate assembly and dispersal times and the duration of the actual parade
- notify police of road closure requirements
- make sure a vet is on hand if animals are participating
- identify a finishing place sufficiently large to hold the parade participants and spectators. Make sure that if there

are gates to the area that they are sufficiently wide for parade lorries to enter and that there is a large enough turning area for the lorries

- if the weather has been wet for a period before the parade, ensure that there is a supply of temporary road surfacing to avoid lorries and other vehicles getting stuck in the mud
- employ ambulance services
- link with the aviation authorities to stage a parade 'flypast'
- do you require civic involvement?
- make VIP arrangements for sponsors/local dignitaries
- do you need to build a viewing platorm for VIPs/sponsors?
- will you require street entertainers to perform alongside the parade?
- will there be street traders/food sellers along the parade route?
- allow approximately one mile per hour as the parade travelling time
- notify public transport companies, including taxis, that their timetables may be slightly disrupted on the day of the parade
- notify the following local authority departments: leisure, planning, licensing, environmental health, direct services, mayor's office
- contact local press, radio, TV
- employ the services of stewards for crowd management, to walk at the side of the parade and in the assembly and arrival areas
- consider what you want to happen in the area where the parade arrives - a horse show? A family fun day?
- ensure that you have good two-way communication with stewards, other organisers, etc.
- consider all aspects of health and safety

c) opening and closing ceremonies

You might want to consider employing a professional productions company to organise your opening and closing ceremonies. Otherwise you need to consider:

- timings and sequences
- rehearsal arrangements
- costumes
- flags and accessories
- balloons and inflatables
- minor works and construction
- musical arrangement
- theme songs
- choice
- sound effects
- sound track reproduction
- special effects
- choreography
- artistic, creative and lighting
- personnel and training
- budget and expenditure
- professional production
- key players
- master of ceremonies
- VIPs
- participants

d) protocol and VIP accommodation

You might want to consider:

- arrival and welcome
- baggage
- handbook manual
- registration
- protocol office
- protocol staff
- venue protocol
- hospitality
- victory VIP ceremonies/presentations
- VIP roll call
- Royal visit
- receptions and functions
- hotel accommodation
- accreditation
- ticketing and seating
- gold passes and car parking
- transport
- lounges
- toilets
- information
- liaison
- accompanying personnel
- departure

e) swimming event – example event requirements form

EVENT INFORMATION					
Name of organising group					
Contact name					
Address					
Telephone Business		Mobile		Home	
Fax		E-mail			

Event title			**Event date**	

Times	Entry to changing room		Warm up	
	Gala starts		Gala finishes	

Numbers anticipated	Guests		Officials	
	Swimmers		Spectators	
	Special guests			

Reserved seats	How many?		Poolside for presentation of trophies	
	Overlooking pool		Finish	
	Shallow end		Second pool	

Music and PA requirements	Nature and time required		Location of microphone(s)	

Catering numbers	Type of catering		Meal	
	Guests		Officials	
	Competitors		Time(s) required	
	Anticipated costs			

Additional rooms	State no		Use and time	

Additional information (special requirements for guests, sponsors etc)	

Poolside requirements	Number of lanes		Starting block nos – deep end	
	Number of chairs		Timekeepers – deep	
	Turn judges – boom		Finish judges – deep	
	Competitors – shallow		Competitors – deep	
	False start ropes		Referee/starter chairs	
	Announcers table/ chair/microphone		Trophy table	
	Backstroke flags		Recorders table/chairs	
	Computer table		Winner's podium	

Additional information (ie timing pads, advertising banners etc)	

Pool layout	Please indicate preferred layout using diagram. Send copy of diagram to floor manager, pool supervisor etc

f) fun run

The definition of a fun run is that prizes are not given according to finishing position. Thus, everybody may be given a medal, or a spot prize may be handed out, but the winner is not given a trophy or prize.

In fact, this definition has become blurred and many fun runs elect to provide prizes of one kind or another. The advice given below is therefore more relevant to organisers of all running events.

Firstly, it is essential to be clear of your event's objectives before proceeding. Therefore, you must ask yourself 'what is the event's primary objective?' For example, is it:

- to raise money for charity? If so, a short distance event in a local park may be appropriate.
- to raise awareness of your organisation? A high-profile event with good quality medals provided is essential.
- to promote your running club? An accurately measured route starting and finishing near your club facilities is ideal.
- to add a good quality, well organised run to support the local running scene?

The checklist provided below is intended to address all possible issues but bear in mind it will be influenced by the following:

- Your objectives
- Your financial resources
- Your staffing resources
- The area where you live

It must be stressed that however you choose to answer the above, the runners' needs must always come first. The course must be safe, be cleared with the appropriate authorities and be adequately marshalled. You must have adequate public liability insurance and there must be sufficient first aid support. These are the basic responsibilities of the fun run organiser. It is advisable to take advice from local runners.

There are specialist suppliers for most of the services listed below. Get advice from others before ordering and get quotations in advance.

Advice – usually free and easily obtainable from your local authority, running club or athletics associations. Make sure you use it!

Athletic club levy – if the event has a British Athletics Federation (BAF) permit (see BAF in Help, Advice and Support chapter 18 in this book), you should charge every unaffiliated runner (i.e. runners who are not members of a BAF registered running club) a £1 levy which is then payable to the BAF.

Banners – you should have start and finish banners and may wish to have some others, e.g. name of event. Decide what logos and wording you want on them.

Bibs – all the event officials should be clearly identified. You may want them to be specific to their jobs, e.g. marshal, event director, etc. Running clubs and local authorities often have supplies which they may loan out.

British Athletics Federation (BAF) Permit – a fun run on its own does not require a permit. However, acquiring a permit will provide the event with public liability cover (via BAF). To get a permit contact your local athletic association and ask for the permit secretary. To get a permit the course must have been measured by a recognised course measurer (if it is promoted as an exact distance, e.g. the kilometre) and you must have consulted the police and the local authority.

NB at the time of writing BAF is in administration and their affairs are being dealt with by UK Athletics '98. However, BAF still regulates road running and issues permits and so it is a BAF permit that is required and it will still provide public liability insurance.

Budget – draft this at the initial planning stages. Make sure you allow for all the essential services and do not be tempted to scrimp on them.

Car Parking – ensure you have space for the number of cars you expect plus the marshals and the signs to make sure they arrive at the right place. Bear in mind you may need parking for your number of runners divided by two (i.e. 250 spaces for 500 runners). Publicise public transport alternatives when available.

Catering – even small runs may have sandwiches and hot drinks for sale. Not only is this a useful service for the runners and spectators, it may also be a money-raising exercise benefiting a local charity. Remember to cater for special dietary requirements.

Commentary – a good commentator will enhance the atmosphere of the event and help keep everybody informed. Ensure they have all relevant information about the event and a list of the runners' name and numbers (in numerical order). An assistant to help the commentator spot runners' names is also useful.

Date – you should avoid a clash with any other relevant local and significant national events (e.g. FA Cup Finals). Check local holidays and half-terms as well. Ensure the venue is available when you want it.

Deadlines – these will depend to some extent on the nature and objectives of your event. For example, a major fun run aiming to attract large numbers must be planned almost a year in advance whereas a low-key club event can be left a bit later.

You should work back from the date of the event and write in the deadline dates when the tasks must be completed. Don't forget that in the real world there are usually delays and you must allow for these in your planning.

Distance – fun runs tend to be any distance up to four miles. Above this is not really suitable for the 'occasional' runner and would be attractive mainly to regular runners who may not be your main target market. For children it must be a lot shorter. Therefore, refer to your main objectives and select the most appropriate distance. Take advice from others, such as a running club. The BAF stipulate the maximum distance children should run. The distance may be determined to an extent by the venue location and the length of course available.

Drinks – these must be provided at the finish. Water is the preferred option. Sweeter drinks such as orange squash need to be diluted more than usual. Tea and coffee should be provided for spectators as well as being popular with the runners on a cold day. Public health requirements should always be kept in mind and bottled drinks will be the safest to provide. Ensure you have enough for two per runner. A drinks station on the course will be needed for runs longer than 5km. They should be placed every 5km in these cases. Do not forget the litter implications.

Entry fees – make this value for money if all proceeds are going to charity.

Entry forms and posters – your promotional material should always contain the following information: name of event, date, start time, venue, entry fee, how you can enter, contact name, address and daytime telephone number and sponsors' logos. The entry form should allow you to receive the follow information from the entrant: name, address, age, sex, athletic club number, contact telephone number – plus anything that's relevant to your event.

Entry processing – make this computerised if possible. You must allow for a last minute rush of entries. If you keep the database of entries you can use it to mail out entry forms for next year's event.

Equipment – make a list of all the items you will need; you will find you keep adding to it! For example, tape, lump hammer, fencing pins, air-horn, clipboards, pens, stopwatches, cups, cable ties and so on.

First Aid – essential you do not cut corners with this. As an absolute minimum you should have first aiders at the finish. Depending on communication and ease of access, there may be other points on the course where they should be sited. Take the advice of the organisation you use (e.g. St. John Ambulance, Red Cross, paramedics). Ask around for the best one locally as the quality and reputation of the voluntary organisations varies from area to area. Make sure you give them a suitable donation.

Information – it is usually helpful to mail out runners' information prior to the event to all pre-entries. It should answer the questions the runners would have, e.g. venue, facilities available, time they need to report by, car parking, route and venue map and so one, plus any information specific to the event. You may also want to include their number and a sponsor form.

Main site – you will need to identify/arrange the following: toilets (will cause complaints if not sufficient), car parking, PA system, (to keep people entertained, informed and relay important messages), registration point, changing rooms/area, signage, prize presentation point, tables and chairs. Additional facilities, such as a baggage store and refreshments, may also be appropriate to your event. Draw a site plan. Have a wet weather alternative plan.

Marshals – there should be sufficient marshals to direct and assist runners. They should wear conspicuous tabards or bibs. Make sure they are well briefed (in advance) as to their duties and responsibilities, have any items of equipment (eg walkie-talkies) they need and are in position in plenty of time. They should not direct traffic – that is the role of the police. Avoid using children except for tasks such as handing out medals and drinks at the finish. Do not forget to thank them and, if budget allows, give them a T-shirt or equivalent.

Medals (and ribbons) – decide what you want to give and budget accordingly. For example, a specially designed medal and ribbon or buy an off-the-shelf one. Note that medals may require up to eight weeks from place of order to delivery, so you may well have to estimate the quantity required.

Miscellaneous – do you want to arrange some extras such as an aerobic warm-up, bouncy castle, entertainment, etc?

Numbers – decide on your numbering system and order appropriate quantities and number sequences. If you have a main sponsor ensure their name (and/or logo) is printed on them. Check delivery times with the supplier. Ensure you have some spares and blanks. Do not forget to get safety pins as well: runners often turn up without them.

Officials – an event with a BAF permit can request a referee, a chief timekeeper, recorders and a starter. Remember they may be in high demand so early booking is essential if required.

On the day – equipment – meet the suppliers on arrival to ensure they are sited correctly. Prepare all the items you require in plenty of time.

On the day – staff – your action plan should highlight the staffing required. As an absolute minimum you need people to take responsibility for the following areas:

- enquiries/registration desk
- the start

- the finish
- marshalling

The event organiser should not allocate him/herself with specific duties. They need to be immediately available in case of any problems or emergencies.

Post event – it is not all over once the runners are finished. You will need to write thank you letters, send out results, issue press releases, pay invoices and tidy up all equipment.

Prize presentations – try to do these on the day and as soon as possible after the finish. The longer the prize list the longer it will take to check the results prior to the presentation. It helps to have an assistant to help with the presentation. Decide if you want a VIP/sponsor to give out the prizes. Remember what was said in the introduction about the definition of a fun run, however.

Programme – these can be time consuming to do and are only necessary for large events (2000+entrants). Some companies specialise at putting programmes together through advertising sales.

Promotion – distribute your entry forms as widely as possible, eg at running clubs, sports shops, other runs, schools, etc. Ensure you send information to relevant 'What's On' columns and event listings at the right time (remember they may have copy deadlines several months in advance of your run). Do not forget to issue press releases and invite the local media on the day. Take photographs which you can use afterwards for the local press and for promotion the following year.

Public address system – this is recommended to keep people informed, entertained and to pass on important messages. Have a pre-event site meeting with the supplier to ascertain your requirements and location.

Public liability insurance – essential

Radio communications – you need to be able to communicate to your staff and around the course. Use either walkie-talkies or mobile phones but check reception beforehand. Communications groups could be used for course communication.

Registration – unless entries are accepted on the day (for fun runs only), registration points should only be provided for enquiries, safety pins, etc.

Results – If you are producing results (strictly speaking, not for fun runs) it is recommended to use a results service or at least someone who is experienced and reliable. Ensure they are sited where the runners can't interrupt them. Computerised systems are essential for all but the smallest runs. You may want to provide envelopes for runners to put their name and address on and leave with fifty pence for results to be sent to them.

Route – ideally it will be on closed roads or in a traffic-free area (this is a definite requirement for children's events). If you must use roads you must liaise with the police and the local authority. Go for an anti-clockwise course to minimise road crossings. You may decide to do laps but do not have more than three (less for shorter than a two mile run). A loop course is easier to manage than a point-to-point or out-and-back.

Rules – at the initial planning decide on the event rules and items such as age categories, team prizes (and number to count) and set out definitions, eg what is meant by a 'local runner'.

Runners with special needs – you will have entrants and spectators with special needs. These may vary from athletes using wheelchairs to blind runners. Ensure your route, facilities (including toilets and signage) are as accessible as possible. If in doubt, seek advice from your local authority or a local sports club run by disabled people.

Signage – used for the route, around the main site and for finding the venue. Distance markers can also be used although take care if using a lap course that they are not confusing. Designs on a fluorescent background are the most effective.

Sponsors – as well as trying for cash, do not forget to look for help in kind. For example, a garage may supply a lead car. Remember to acknowledge this support and to write to them formally afterwards.

Start and finish – allow sufficient space and for ease of movement through. Have an event clock under the gantry if appropriate. Use banners to highlight them.

T-shirts – if you choose to have T-shirts make sure they are of a reasonable quality. It is counter-productive to provide shirts which fade or shrink in the first wash. This is a very competitive field so check out a number of suppliers and prices in advance. Ask to see samples before ordering.

Timekeeping – arrange timekeepers and number recorders, if necessary. They should work in pairs. Arrange recording equipment (watches, clipboards, waterproof covers, recording sheets, pencils).

Toilets – essential and do not forget there is a concentrated period just prior to the run when they are in big demand. Ensure you have plenty for the expected number of runs and spectators.

Trophies and prizes – if it is a fun run make sure that prizes are spread throughout the field.

g) street entertainment

Street art is one of the most popular and innovative art forms in mainland Europe. Each year large-scale street arts festivals are produced across the continent presenting art of the highest quality from professional performers.

Street art is the most celebratory, accessible and all - embracing of art forms incorporating traditional and contemporary music and dance, circus, theatre, mime, visual art, carnival arts, pyrotechnics and new technologies.

The last ten years has seen a rapid increase in the quantity and quality of street art and street art events in this country. This is the artform of the twenty-first century.

There are a number of fundamental issues which prospective producers should bear in mind when planning a street art event.

i) programme

An imaginative and innovative approach should be taken to programming to avoid the cries of "Oh no, not another juggler!" at your event. Recent events have seen contemporary dance in wheelchairs in Bristol City Centre and flamenco on the streets of Lewisham. Both of these performances were great successes and there is something magical about presenting the unexpected in an everyday environment. Street art is also a great social ambassador. Work with local professional artists and community groups to develop performances unique to your locality.

As audiences become more educated there is more pressure on the producer to offer high quality. This can only be a good thing. You can lessen the risk of presenting inappropriate or poor performance by maintaining a policy of only programming shows that you have seen or by employing the services of a reputable specialist street arts producer or agency to programme the event for you. This is especially true in the case of presenting international work which tends to be more expensive and production-intensive than UK work. It is never advisable to be tempted to sacrifice quality of performance for quantity. The public will be more likely to remember one amazing performance than five insignificant shows.

Artist availability can affect the quality of programme that you can present. The availability of the most successful artists becomes a problem in the busy summer season and the situation is unlikely to get any better.

Artists should be matched to the site and the prospective audience. Choose the site very carefully and consider factors such as artist's technical provision, shelter for the audience and the performers, audience sightlines, pedestrian and vehicle traffic routes, proximity to artist dressing rooms, acoustics and noise interference from nearby roads and businesses.

An artist's technical requirements should be considered before a programme is finalised as they will certainly have an important effect on the overall event budget. A basic technical provision can sometimes double the performer's fee.

Most artists will have a clear printed sheet detailing their

technical requirements. This should include details such as:

- minimum size of performance space and any special site requirements, i.e. vehicle access, no balconies, whether the show is performed front-on or in the round and so on
- duration of show and the number of times it can be performed
- power requirements
- whether a PA is needed and who should supply it
- dressing room requirements
- parking requirements
- security provision: it may be that overnight security is required
- details of get-in and get-out times
- what accommodation and food should be provided by the producer.

If an artist does not have a specific list of requirements it is advisable to go through each of these items with them and confirm them in writing. Technical provision details often form part of the producer/artist contract.

ii) liaison

Maintaining close liaison between all the disparate groups involved in a street arts event is absolutely crucial to the safe and successful production of an event. The producer's role is to ensure the reliability and clarity of all information and that it is communicated to all necessary parties prior to the event.

iii) artists

There should be a signed contract between the artists and the producer clearly stating the rights and duties of each party. This will prevent any misunderstandings in the event of a later incident. The artists should also be sent clear details well in advance of the event including a map indicating access, performance space, dressing rooms and allocated parking spaces; a performance schedule; confirmation of agreed technical provision; background details of the event including any print marketing; an agreed arrival time and the name and contact number of the producer's on-site representative.

If the performance is a large-scale show that may present production difficulties, e.g. if it contains pyrotechnics, then a site visit between the producer, the artist and the relevant authorities (see below) should be arranged well in advance of the event. This is especially true for international companies and is well worth the extra expense. Happy artists equal a happy event.

iv) authorities

There are many different authorities and agencies that need to be considered in the pre-production of an event that will take place in a busy public place.

The authorities to contact will vary according to the size of the event but do consider the following:

- the local authority
- environmental health
- licensing
- leisure services department
- police
- fire services
- first aid
- town centre manager
- shopping centre management
- local traders' assocation
- local residents' association

If road closures are needed you should also work with the Traffic and Highways Department and be sure to notify bus and taxi operators and any sections of the public who are likely to be affected.

The best way to inform all the relevant authorities is to produce and circulate an event manual as soon as the programme is finalised. This document should include background details about the event, details of the performance site(s), performance and production schedule, details of technical provision, information about the artists that will be performing, details of any road closures, contact details of the producers, risk assessments and ways in which the risks will be dealt with: provision of stewards, fire extinguishers, hand held radios, emergency evacuation procedures crowd control and so on.

After the event manual has been circulated an initial round-table meeting should be arranged. This provides the authorities with the opportunity to ask any questions and make any additional suggestions. These recommendations should be incorporated into the revised event manual. Again, this should be circulated and a final round-table meeting arranged just prior to the event.

Finally, the practical information from this last meeting should be bound into an operational document for use by the event team, with relevant production schedule, site maps, contact details, event personnel information and radio procedures.

v) wet weather

The British audience is heartier than you may think when it comes to enjoying themselves. You should work out your wet weather policy as early as possible and incorporate this into the artist contract and the event manual.

Always remember that if an artist has turned up they want to perform and will do so unless it presents a serious risk to life or limb to continue.

One way to prevent a complete washout is to locate an alternative venue in the case of wet weather: an indoor shopping centre or community centre. If you do decide to do this ensure that you include this somewhere on your publicity and that resilient stewards remain in the original venue to direct the audience to the new performance site. A-boards are invaluable at a time like this.

Remember the following points:

- be careful in your choice of site
- stress quality and range of work in your programming
- always choose a programme that is suitable to the site and potential audience
- ensure you have an experienced, friendly event team and that they are briefed about the event so they can inform the public
- market and publicise the event dully and effectively
- ensure that you produce a clear and concise event manual and stick with it
- you have the opportunity to create a high-quality celebratory arts event that brings the whole community together

This information was produced by Dave Reeves, Director at Zap Productions, which has organised successful large and small-scale outdoor events since 1989. You can find more information about Zap Productions at the back of this book.

h) volunteer checklist

- ☐ identification
- ☐ sources
- ☐ recruitment
- ☐ training
- ☐ management
- ☐ motivation
- ☐ reward
- ☐ recognition
- ☐ catering
- ☐ accreditation
- ☐ transport
- ☐ mementos
- ☐ role/responsibility

i) entertainment checklist

- [ ] acrobats
- [ ] after dinner speakers
- [ ] archery
- [ ] bagpipers
- [ ] ballet dancers
- [ ] barbershop singers
- [ ] barn dance
- [ ] big bands
- [ ] brass bands
- [ ] break dancing
- [ ] cabaret
- [ ] carollers
- [ ] cartoonist
- [ ] casinos
- [ ] ceilidh bands
- [ ] celebrities
- [ ] choirs
- [ ] clay pigeon shooting
- [ ] clowns/jesters
- [ ] comedians
- [ ] contortionists
- [ ] dance troupes
- [ ] dancing
- [ ] disc jockeys
- [ ] discos
- [ ] dog displays
- [ ] escapologists
- [ ] face/body painting
- [ ] falconry
- [ ] fairground
- [ ] fire eaters
- [ ] flamenco music/dance

- [ ] fortune tellers
- [ ] gladiator jousts
- [ ] graphologists
- [ ] harpists
- [ ] hypnotists
- [ ] illusionists
- [ ] jazz bands
- [ ] jousting
- [ ] jugglers
- [ ] karaoke
- [ ] laser clays
- [ ] latin bands
- [ ] limbo dancers
- [ ] line dancing
- [ ] look-alikes/soundalikes
- [ ] mime artists
- [ ] minstrels
- [ ] mock battles
- [ ] morris dancers
- [ ] motor cycle displays
- [ ] murder mystery
- [ ] music hall shows
- [ ] orchestras
- [ ] paintball
- [ ] pianist
- [ ] psychic
- [ ] Punch & Judy
- [ ] puppeteers
- [ ] quad bikes
- [ ] quizzes
- [ ] race nights
- [ ] robots
- [ ] rodeo bull
- [ ] scalextric

- [ ] Scottish piper
- [ ] silhouette cutting
- [ ] simulators
- [ ] singing/crazy waiters
- [ ] steel band
- [ ] stilt walkers
- [ ] string quartets
- [ ] stuntmen
- [ ] sword swallowers
- [ ] table magicians
- [ ] tap dancers
- [ ] tea dances
- [ ] town criers
- [ ] trapeze artists
- [ ] tribute bands
- [ ] ventriloquists
- [ ] videos

j) various types of venues

- [ ] airports
- [ ] arenas
- [ ] art galleries
- [ ] arts centres
- [ ] boats (permanently moored – or not!)
- [ ] civic centres/town halls
- [ ] community centres
- [ ] conference centres
- [ ] football/rugby grounds
- [ ] golf clubs
- [ ] holiday camps
- [ ] hotels
- [ ] leisure centres/clubs
- [ ] museums

- [ ] racecourses
- [ ] science parks
- [ ] stadia
- [ ] theme parks
- [ ] theatres
- [ ] travel lodges
- [ ] universities/colleges
- [ ] visitor attractions
- [ ] Zoos

k)   master events checklist

- [ ] access times
- [ ] accessibility
- [ ] accommodation
- [ ] accounts
- [ ] accreditation
- [ ] acoustics
- [ ] administration
- [ ] admissions
- [ ] advertising
- [ ] agencies
- [ ] agents
- [ ] aims
- [ ] alcohol
- [ ] ancillary activities
- [ ] ancillary facilities
- [ ] announcements
- [ ] appeals for funds
- [ ] appeals for volunteers
- [ ] application forms
- [ ] arrival/departure times
- [ ] artistes
- [ ] artwork
- [ ] atmosphere

- [ ] audience
- [ ] audio visual requirements
- [ ] audit
- [ ] badges
- [ ] banking
- [ ] banners
- [ ] barriers
- [ ] big screen hire
- [ ] blackout facilities
- [ ] bookings
- [ ] box office
- [ ] budgeting procedures
- [ ] business plan
- [ ] calor gas
- [ ] cancellation
- [ ] car parking
- [ ] cash collection
- [ ] cash flow/change
- [ ] catering
- [ ] ceremonies
- [ ] certificates
- [ ] chairperson
- [ ] chairs and tables
- [ ] changing rooms
- [ ] charities
- [ ] checklists
- [ ] children
- [ ] children's act
- [ ] church services
- [ ] civic/government receptions
- [ ] cleaners
- [ ] cloakrooms
- [ ] colour themes
- [ ] commentators

- [ ] committees
- [ ] communications
- [ ] community
- [ ] competitors
- [ ] complaints procedures
- [ ] complimentary tickets
- [ ] computers
- [ ] concessions
- [ ] contingency plans
- [ ] contractors
- [ ] contracts
- [ ] control centre
- [ ] copyright
- [ ] crèche
- [ ] critical path
- [ ] crowd management and flow
- [ ] currency rates
- [ ] customer care
- [ ] date
- [ ] debriefing
- [ ] decoration
- [ ] delegates
- [ ] demonstrations
- [ ] departure arrangements
- [ ] dietery requirements
- [ ] diplomacy
- [ ] direct mailshots
- [ ] hosts/hostesses
- [ ] disabled facilities
- [ ] display boards
- [ ] displays
- [ ] documentation
- [ ] donations
- [ ] drainage

- [ ] dressing rooms
- [ ] drug testing
- [ ] duty of care
- [ ] electrical supply
- [ ] electricians
- [ ] electricity
- [ ] e-mail
- [ ] emergency procedures
- [ ] emergency services
- [ ] enquiries
- [ ] entertainment
- [ ] entrances
- [ ] entry arrangements
- [ ] equipment
- [ ] estimates - income/expenditure
- [ ] evaluation (post event)
- [ ] event handbook
- [ ] exchange facilities
- [ ] exhibitions
- [ ] exhibits
- [ ] exits
- [ ] facilities at venue
- [ ] facsimile
- [ ] feasibility study
- [ ] fees
- [ ] fencing
- [ ] films
- [ ] financial planning policy
- [ ] fire regulations
- [ ] fireworks
- [ ] first aid
- [ ] flags
- [ ] float of small change
- [ ] floral decorations

- [ ] food hygiene backstage
- [ ] franchise arrangements
- [ ] fund raising
- [ ] gas
- [ ] general public
- [ ] gifts
- [ ] grant aid
- [ ] greeting
- [ ] ground conditions
- [ ] guests
- [ ] health & safety act
- [ ] hiring
- [ ] hospitality
- [ ] hosting
- [ ] hotels
- [ ] identification
- [ ] image
- [ ] income/expenditure
- [ ] information
- [ ] insurance
- [ ] internet interpreters interviews
- [ ] invitations
- [ ] invoicing
- [ ] lasers
- [ ] lecterns
- [ ] legal considerations
- [ ] letters
- [ ] liaison officers
- [ ] licenses
- [ ] lifeguards
- [ ] lighting
- [ ] litter collection
- [ ] loading/unloading facilities
- [ ] local authority

- [ ] location
- [ ] logos
- [ ] lost children
- [ ] lost property
- [ ] lotteries
- [ ] maintenance
- [ ] manpower
- [ ] maps
- [ ] market research
- [ ] marketing
- [ ] marquees
- [ ] master of ceremonies
- [ ] medals
- [ ] media
- [ ] medical provision
- [ ] meeting plans
- [ ] menus
- [ ] merchandising
- [ ] message board
- [ ] messages
- [ ] microphones
- [ ] mission statement
- [ ] mobile phones
- [ ] monitoring
- [ ] music requirements
- [ ] newspapers
- [ ] noise
- [ ] no-shows
- [ ] numbers participating
- [ ] objectives
- [ ] offices
- [ ] officials
- [ ] organisational plan
- [ ] participants

- [ ] partnerships
- [ ] passes
- [ ] patents
- [ ] patronage
- [ ] performers
- [ ] performing rights
- [ ] permits
- [ ] photocall
- [ ] photocopier
- [ ] photography
- [ ] pit areas
- [ ] planning
- [ ] plans
- [ ] policing
- [ ] political support
- [ ] post-event arrangements
- [ ] poster sites
- [ ] power supply
- [ ] practice facilities
- [ ] presentations
- [ ] press
- [ ] press conference
- [ ] press launch
- [ ] press releases
- [ ] press room
- [ ] prestigious supports
- [ ] pricing policy
- [ ] printed programme
- [ ] printing
- [ ] prizes
- [ ] programme
- [ ] promotion

- [ ] protective clothing
- [ ] protocol
- [ ] public address system
- [ ] public consultation
- [ ] public liability
- [ ] public relations
- [ ] public transport
- [ ] publicity
- [ ] radio
- [ ] raffles
- [ ] receipt systems
- [ ] reception areas
- [ ] recycling
- [ ] refreshment breaks
- [ ] refunds
- [ ] refuse areas and disposal
- [ ] registration
- [ ] rehearsals
- [ ] religious services
- [ ] reporting systems
- [ ] research
- [ ] reservations
- [ ] resources
- [ ] results board
- [ ] retail outlets
- [ ] risk assessment
- [ ] safety
- [ ] sales
- [ ] schedules
- [ ] scoreboards

- [ ] seating
- [ ] seating arrangements
- [ ] secretarial services
- [ ] security
- [ ] services (electricity, etc)
- [ ] shops
- [ ] signage
- [ ] signposting
- [ ] sound
- [ ] sound checks
- [ ] soundproofing
- [ ] souvenirs
- [ ] speakers
- [ ] spectators
- [ ] spectators' arrangements
- [ ] sponsors
- [ ] sponsorship
- [ ] staff/stewards
- [ ] staging
- [ ] stall holders
- [ ] stationery
- [ ] stewarding
- [ ] stock checking
- [ ] stock checks
- [ ] storage
- [ ] strategies
- [ ] street entertainment
- [ ] structures (or organisation)
- [ ] subsistence
- [ ] Sunday trading law

- [ ] support services
- [ ] swot analysis
- [ ] tasks
- [ ] taxis/coaches
- [ ] team liaison
- [ ] technical equipment
- [ ] technical requirements
- [ ] technicians
- [ ] technology
- [ ] telephone
- [ ] telephone sales
- [ ] teletext
- [ ] television
- [ ] tents
- [ ] thank yous

- [ ] ticketing
- [ ] tickets
- [ ] timetable
- [ ] toilets
- [ ] tombola
- [ ] top table
- [ ] tourist services
- [ ] traders/exhibitors
- [ ] traffic control
- [ ] training
- [ ] transport
- [ ] travel (agents)
- [ ] triage
- [ ] trophies
- [ ] two-way radios

- [ ] uniform
- [ ] ushers
- [ ] value added tax
- [ ] venue(s)
- [ ] vips
- [ ] visitor facilities
- [ ] visual scoring
- [ ] volunteers
- [ ] warm up
- [ ] waste disposal
- [ ] weater supplies
- [ ] weather contingencies
- [ ] welfare
- [ ] wheelchair hire
- [ ] work schedules

l) indoor venue inspection forms

INDOOR VENUE INSPECTION FORM – 1					
Venue					
Location					
Address					
			Postcode		
Contact name					
Tel no		Fax no			
Email		Website			
Signature of Inspector					
Is the venue easy to find?	YES			NO	
Name and distance of nearest railway					
Nearest tube line and station					
Is car parking available?	YES			NO	
Free or Pay & Display	Free			P & D	
Is there a hotel courtesy coach?	YES			NO	
Is there access for delegates in wheelchairs?	YES			NO	
Are guide dogs for the visually impaired allowed in the venue?	YES			NO	

INDOOR VENUE INSPECTION FORM – 2

MEETING ROOMS *(you will need one form for each meeting room)*

Name of room						
Is the lighting natural or artificial?						
Are emergency exit instructions available?	YES			NO		
Is there likely to be any noise either inside or outside the building, ie from the kitchens or from external refurbishment work?						
Draw a basic picture of the room including power sockets/emergency exits, etc	Picture:					
Are there any pillars/columns?	YES			NO		
Are there any mirrors?	YES			NO		
Are there any windows?	YES			NO		
Is there a blackout facility and if so, is this adequate?	YES			NO		
Is the room partitioned?	YES			NO		
Is the partition soundproofed?	YES			NO		
Is staging available?	YES			NO		
If so, what size is the staging?						
Is there a cost for the staging?	YES			NO		
Is a lectern available?	YES			NO		
If so, is there a charge for the lectern?	£					
What is the maximum capacity of the room in the following style of layouts:						
Theatre						
Classroom						
U-shape						
Boardroom						
Banquet						
Herringbone						
Horseshoe						
Is it possible for you to see the room in use?	YES			NO		

INDOOR VENUE INSPECTION FORM – 3

EQUIPMENT – Is the following equipment available?

PA system	YES			NO	
Loop hearing system (if yes, where?)	YES			NO	
Is there space for back projection?	YES			NO	
Is there a facility to record the proceedings?	YES			NO	
Is there a technician available onsite?	YES			NO	
Name of venue's preferred contractors, if any:					
Costs charged by preferred contractors are:					
Where is the lights control box?					
Can lights be dimmed?	YES			NO	
Heating system – is it noisy?	YES			NO	
Air conditioning – is it noisy?	YES			NO	
Is the seating comfortable?	YES			NO	
If seating is not comfortable, what can be done about it?					

CATERING

Name of room:					
Is it close to/same level as meeting room(s)?					
Maximum capacity for a seated meal?					
Maximum capacity for a standing meal?					
What is the suggested table layout?					
What is the maximum number of serving points? (Recommend 2 serving points per 50 delegates)					
Speed of service for seated hot/cold lunch?					
Speed of service for standing hot/cold lunch?					
Will a copy of the menu be available in advance?	YES			NO	
Is private dining available?	YES			NO	
Is a cash bar available?	YES			NO	

INDOOR VENUE INSPECTION FORM – 4

OTHER FACILITIES

Is a Conference Organisers' office available?	YES			NO		
If yes, name of room?						
Number and location of toilets						
What is the general standard of cleanliness throughout the venue?						
What local shops are within walking distance? ie pharmacy, newsagents, etc						
Name and telephone number of local taxi company						

BEDROOMS

Number of single rooms available?						
Number of double rooms available?						
Number of twin rooms available?						
Number of suites available?						
Number of rooms suitable for disabled people?						
How many smoking rooms available?						
How many non-smoking rooms available?						
What is the size of the bedroom and bathroom?						
What time can people check in?						
What is checkout time?						
Is there a minibar in the room?	YES			NO		
Is there a hair dryer?	YES			NO		
Is there a trouser press?	YES			NO		
Is tea/coffee available in the room?	YES			NO		
Is a desk or table available in the room?	YES			NO		
Is satellite television available in the room?	YES			NO		
Are the leisure facilties free of charge to residents?	YES			NO		
What might cause noise nuisance?						
Is room service available?	YES			NO		
Is breakfast included in the rate?	YES			NO		
If so, what is the price of breakfast?						
Is there an internet link in bedrooms?	YES			NO		
If not, is there an internet link anywhere in the building?	YES			NO		
If yes, where is it located?						

INDOOR VENUE INSPECTION FORM – 5

GENERAL

Is additional signage necessary?	YES			NO	
If additional signage is necessary, how many signs and where should these be located?					
Can signage/posters/exhibition stands be erected in the venue?					
What method of fixing is allowed?					
Will any refurbishment work be taking place during the Conference?	YES			NO	
If yes, when and where?					
Is there good access to all areas for delegates and AV crew? ie lifts, stairs, ramps, etc	YES			NO	
If access is not good, what can be done about it?					

BEFORE YOU LEAVE

Obtain a full list of hire charges for all rooms/facilities	
Obtain a copy of the Terms & Conditions and Cancellation Policy	
Ask for a location map and written travel instructions	
Ask for a hotel brochure	
Obtain a business card of your contact	
Obtain a copy of the venue's emergency evacuation procedures	
Ask for a selection of menus and prices	

chapter seventeen
not quite the end...

The authors are aware that not every aspect of event management is covered in this book. The subject is very diverse, with most events being a one-off experience, but we have tried to cover the fundamental principles of event management.

Having drawn upon the wisdom of this text, you should now be better placed to organise your events. That said, you will not know everything and never will – nobody ever does!

You will still need to plan carefully and if you do not know something – ask someone – perhaps one of the contributors to this book all of whom we can highly recommend to you. Do not make your own mistakes, that is not the best way to learn.

This text is best used to dip into on an 'as and when' basis, to help you remember, to inform, to refresh your memory about various aspects of event organisation. We can all do it better with the advice and support of others.

Event organisation is great fun and very rewarding if done properly; that comes through knowledge, hard work and experience.

The fundamental message is:
• Know what and why you are doing it
• Plan
• Pay attention to detail
• Deliver for your customers
• Evaluate your performance

The authors wish you well in your event organising career – the following chapter will help you.

> "I always pass on good advice. It is the only thing to do with it. It is never of any use to oneself"
>
> *(Oscar Wilde 1854 – 1900)*

chapter eighteen

help, advice and support

a) helpful organisations

Arts Council for Northern Ireland (The)
MacNeice House
77 Malone Road
Belfast BT9 6AQ
Tel: 028 90 385200
Fax: 028 90 661715
www.artscouncil-ni.org

Arts Council England
14 Great Peter Street
London SW1P 3NQ
Tel: 020 7333 0100
Fax: 020 7973 6590
www.artscouncil.org.uk

Arts Council of Northern Ireland
MacNeice House
77 Malone Road
Belfast BT9 6AQ
Tel: 028 9038 5200
Fax: 028 9066 1715
www.artscouncil-ni.org

Arts Council of Wales
Central Office
9 Museum Place
Cardiff CF10 3NX
Tel: 029 20 376500
Fax: 029 20 221447
E-mail:
feedback@artswales.org.uk
www.artswales.org

Arts and Business
Nutmeg House
60 Gainsford Street
Butler's Wharf
London SE1 2NY
Tel: 020 7378 8143
Fax: 020 7407 7527
www.aandb.org.uk

Association for Conferences and Events
Riverside House
High Street
Huntingdon
Cambridgeshire PE18 6SG
Tel: 01480 457595
Fax: 01480 412863
www.martex.co.uk/ace

Association of Exhibition Organisers (The)
113 High Street
Berkhamsted
Hertfordshire HP4 2DJ
Tel: 01442 873331
Fax: 01442 875551
www.aeo.org.uk

Automobile Association
Contact Centre
Carr Ellison House
William Armstrong Drive
Newcastle upon Tyne NE4 7YA
Tel: 0870 600 0371
Fax: 0191 235 5111
www.theaa.com

AVT Limited
AVT House
Stone Street
Brighton BN1 2HB
Tel: 01273 299001
Fax: 01273 299002
www.avtgroup.com

Boldscan Limited
Tonedale Mills
Wellington
Somerset TA21 0AB
Tel: 01823 665849
Fax: 01823 665850
www.boldscan.com

British Association of Conference Destinations
6th Floor, Charles House
148-149 Great Charles Street
Birmingham B3 3HT
Tel: 0121 212 1400
Fax: 0121 212 3131
www.bacd.org.uk

British Athletics Federation
www.british-athletics.co.uk

British Council (The)
10 Spring Gardens
London SW1A 2BN
Tel: 020 7389 3194
Fax: 020 7389 3199
www.britishcouncil.org

British Exhibition Contractors Association (The)
BECA House
Uplands Business Park
Blackhorse Lane
London E17 5QL
Tel: 020 8523 5262
Fax: 020 8523 5204
www.beca.org.uk

British Federation of Festivals
Festivals House
198 Park Lane, Macclesfield
Cheshire SK11 6UD
Tel: 01625 828297
Fax: 01625 503229
www.festivals.demon.co.uk

British Hospitality Association
Queens House
55-56 Lincoln's Inn Fields
London WC2A 3BH
Tel: 020 7404 7744
Fax: 020 7404 7799
www.bha-online.org.uk

British Institute of Professional Photography
Fox Talbot House
Ware, Hertfordshire SG12 9HN
Tel: 01920 464011
Fax: 01920 487056
www.bipp.com

British Olympic Association
1 Wandsworth Plain
London SW18 1EH
Tel: 020 8871 2677
Fax: 020 8871 9104
www.olympics.org.uk

Business in Sport and Leisure Limited
17a Charterfield Avenue
Putney, London SW15 6DX
Tel: 020 8780 2377
Fax: 020 8788 2277
www.bisl.org.uk

CCH Editions Limited
(Croner's Reference Book for VAT)
Croner, CCH Group Ltd
145 London Road
Kingston upon Thames
Surrey KT2 6SR
Tel: 020 8547 3333
Fax: 020 8547 2638
www.croner.cch.co.uk

Central Council of Physical Recreation (CCPR)
Francis House
Francis Street
London SW1P 1DE
Tel: 020 7854 8500
Fax: 020 7854 8501
www.ccpr.org.uk

Charities Aid Foundation
Kings Hill
West Mallow
Kent ME19 4TA
Tel: 01732 520000
Fax: 01732 520001
www.cafonline.org

Charity Commission (The)
Hamsworth House
13-15 Bouverie Street
London EC4Y 8DP
Tel: 0870 333 0123
Fax: 020 7674 2300
www.charity-commission.gov.uk

Chartered Institute of Library and Information Professionals (CILIP)
7 Ridgmont Street
London WC1E 7AE
Tel: 020 7255 0500
Fax: 020 7255 0501
www.cilip.org.uk

Civic Trust (The)
17 Carlton House Terrace
London SW1Y 5AW
Tel: 020 7930 0914
Fax: 020 7321 0180
www.civictrust.org.uk

Community Matters
12-20 Baron Street
London N1 9LL
Tel: 020 7837 7887
Fax: 020 7278 9253
www.communitymatters.org.uk

Complete Talent Agency
200 London Road
Hadleigh
Benfleet, Essex SS7 2PD
Tel: 01702 427100
Fax: 01702 427109
www.entertainers.co.uk

Corporate Hospitality Association
P O Box 67
Kingswood
Hadworth
Surrey KT20 6LG
Tel: 01737 833963
Fax: 01737 833507
www.cha-online.co.uk

Countryside Agency (The)
John Dower House
Crescent Place
Cheltenham
Gloucestershire GL50 3RA
Tel: 01242 521381
Fax: 01242 584270
www.countryside.gov.uk

Countryside Council for Wales (The)
Maes-y-Ffynnon
Penrhosgarnedd
Bangor
Gwynedd LL57 2DW
Tel: 0845 1306229
www.ccw.gov.uk

Crafts Council
44a Pentonville road
Islington
London N1 9BY
Tel: 020 7278 7700
Fax: 020 7837 6891
www.craftscouncil.org.uk

Design Council
34 Bow Street
London WC2E 7DL
Tel: 020 7420 5200
Fax: 020 7420 5300
www.design-council.org.uk

Employers' Organisation for Local Government
Layden House
76-86 Turnmill Street
London EC1M 5LG
Tel: 020 7296 6781
Fax: 020 7296 6750
www.lg-employers.gov.uk

English Heritage
Customer Services Dept.
P O Box 569
Swindon SN2 2YP
Tel: 0870 333 1181
Fax: 01793 414 926
www.english-heritage.org.uk

English Tourism Council / British Tourist Authority
Thames Tower
Black Road
London W6 9EL
Tel: 020 8846 9000
Fax: 020 8563 0302
www.visitbritain.org

Eve Trakway
30/34 Weir Road
Wimbledon
London SW19 8UG
Tel: 020 8879 8807
Fax: 020 8879 8808
www.evetrakway.co.uk

Event Service Association (The)
Centre Court
1301 Stratford Road
Hall Green
Birmingham B28 9HH
Tel: 0121 693 7126
Fax: 0121 693 7100
www.tesa.org.uk

Exhibition Venues Association (EVA)
The National Exhibition Centre
Birmingham B40 1NT
Tel: 0121 767 2758
www.exhibitionvenues.com

**Forestry Commission GB
and Scotland**
Silvan House
231 Corstorphine Road
Edinburgh EH12 7AT
Tel: 0131 334 0303
Fax: 0131 334 3047
www.forestry.gov.uk

Mike Fulford
Leisure Advice
18 Curlew Hill
Morpeth
Northumberland NE61 3SH
Tel: 01670 516843
Email: mikefulford@msn.com

Healthstart Limited
8 Tower Street
Brunswick Business Park
Liverpool L3 4BJ
Tel: 0151 707 2566
Fax: 0870 990 1998
www.healthstart.co.uk

Hospitality Training Foundation
International House
High Street
Ealing
London W5 5DB
Tel: 020 8579 2400
Fax: 020 8840 6217
www.htf.org.uk

**Hotel, Catering and Institutional
Management Association**
191 Trinity Road
London SW17 7HN
Tel: 020 8672 7251
Fax: 020 8682 1707
www.hcima.org.uk

ILAM Services Limited
ILAM House
Lower Basildon
Reading
Berkshire RG8 9NE
Tel: 01491 874850
Fax: 01491 874801
www.ilam.co.uk

**Improvement and Development
Agency for Local Government**
Layden House
76-86 Turnmill Street
London EC1M 5LG
Tel: 020 7296 6600
Fax: 020 7296 6666
www.idea.gov.uk

**Institute of Leisure and Amenity
Management (ILAM)**
ILAM House
Lower Basildon
Reading
Berkshire RG8 9NE
Tel: 01491 874800
Fax: 01491 874801
www.ilam.co.uk

Institute of Management (The)
3rd Floor
2 Savoy Court
The Strand
London WC2R 0EZ
Tel: 020 7497 0580
Fax: 020 7497 0463
www.managers.org.uk

**Institute of Management
Consultants**
3rd Floor
17/18 Hayward's Place
London EC1R 0EQ
Tel: 020 7566 5220
Fax: 020 7566 5230
www.imc.co.uk

Institute of Marketing (The)
Moore Hall
Cookham
Maidenhead
Berkshire SL6 9QH
Tel: 01628 427500
Fax: 01628 427499
www.cim.co.uk

Institute of Public Relations
The Old Trading House
15 Northburgh Street
London EC1V 0PR
Tel: 020 7253 5151
Fax: 020 7490 0588
www.ipr.org.uk

**Institute of Sales and Marketing
Management**
Romeland House
Romeland Hill
St. Albans
Hertfordshire SL3 4ET
Tel: 01727 812500
Fax: 01727 812525
www.ismm.co.uk

**Institute of Sports Sponsorship
(The)**
Warwick House
4th Floor
Buckingham Palace Road
London SW1W 0PP
Tel: 020 7233 7747
Fax: 020 7828 7099
www.sports-sponsorship.co.uk

Institute of Travel and Tourism
Mill Studio
Crane Mead
Ware
Hertfordshire SG12 9PY
Tel: 0870 7707860
Fax: 0870 7707961
www.itt.co.uk

**International Association for
Professional Congress Organisers
(IAPCO)**
42 Canham Road
London W3 7SR
Tel: 020 8749 6171
Fax: 020 8740 0241
www.iapco.org

**International Special Events
Society**
401 North Michigan Avenue
Chicago
IL60611-4267
United States of America
Tel: 312-321-6853
Fax: 312-673-6953
www.ises.com

Kalamazoo Security Print Limited
Northfield
Birmingham B31 2NY
Tel: 0800 454751
Fax: 0121 256 2246
www.kalamazoosolutions.co.uk

Law Society (The)
Law Society's Hall
113 Chancery Lane
London WC2A 1PL
Tel: 020 7242 1222
Fax: 020 7831 0344
www.lawsociety.org.uk

Local Government Association
Local Government House
Smith Square
London SW1P 3HZ
Tel: 020 7664 3131
Fax: 020 7664 3030
www.lga.gov.uk

Market Research Society (The)
15 Northburgh Street
London EC1V 0JR
Tel: 020 7490 4911
Fax: 020 7490 0608
www.mrs.org.uk

Mellor, Penny
Basement Flat
Southern Street
London N1 9AY
Tel: 020 7837 2230
Fax: 020 7833 4988

Mobile and Outside Caterers Association (Great Britain) Limited
Centre Court
1301 Stratford Road
Hall Green
Birmingham B28 9HH
Tel: 0121 693 7000
Fax: 0121 693 7100
www.moca.org.uk

Museums Association (The)
24 Calvin Street
London E1 6NW
Tel: 020 7426 6970
www.museumsassociation.org

Made-Up Textiles Association (The)
42 Heath Street
Tamworth
Staffordshire B79 7JH
Tel: 01827 52337
Fax: 01827 310827
www.muta.org.uk

National Association for Local Councils
109 Great Russell Street
London WC1B 3LD
Tel: 020 7637 1865
Fax: 020 7436 7451
www.nalc.gov.uk

National Exhibitors Association
29 Market Square
Biggleswade
Bedfordshire SG18 8AQ
Tel: 01767 316255
Fax: 01767 316430

Making Music, National Federation of Music Societies
7-15 Rosebery Avenue
London EC1R 4SP
Tel: 0870 903 3780
Fax: 0870 903 3785
www.makingmusic.org.uk

National Outdoor Events Association (The)
7 Hamilton Way
Wallington
Surrey SM6 9NJ
Tel: 020 8669 8121
Fax: 020 8647 1128
www.noea.org.uk

National Playing Fields Association (The)
Stanley House
St. Chad's Place
London WC1X 9HH
Tel: 020 7833 5360
Fax: 020 7833 5365
www.npfa.co.uk

National Trust (The)
36 Queen Anne's Gate
London SW1H 9AS
Tel: 0870 609 5380
Fax: 020 7222 5097
www.nationaltrust.org.uk

National Trust for Scotland (The)
18 Charlotte Square
Edinburgh EH2 4ET
Tel: 0131 243 9300
Fax: 0131 243 9301
www.nts.org.uk

Northern Ireland Tourist Board
59 North Street
Belfast BT1 1NB
Tel: 028 9023 1221
Fax: 028 9024 0960
www.discovernorthernireland.com

Pains Fireworks
The Chalk Pit
Romsey Road
Whiteparish
Salisbury
Wiltshire SP5 2SD
Tel: 01794 884040
Fax: 01794 84015
www.painsfireworks.co.uk

Performing Arts Management Limited
7 Canalside
Clarence Mill
Bollington
Macclesfield
Cheshire SK10 5JZ
Tel: 01625 575681
Fax: 01625 572839
www.performingarts.co.uk

Performing Right Society
29-33 Berners Street
London
W1T 3AB
Tel: 08000 68 48 28
Fax: 0173 331 2712
www.prs.co.uk

Phonographic Performance Ltd
Check address
Tel: 020 7534 1000
www.ppluk.com

Production Services Association
1301 Stratford Road
Hall Green
Birmingham B28 9HH
Tel: 0121 693 7127
Fax: 0121 693 7100
www.psa.org.uk

Regan Cowland Associates
Television Centre
Vinters Park
New Cut Road
Maidstone
Kent ME14 5NZ
Tel: 01622 684 507
Fax: 01622 684 660

Scottish Arts Council (The)
12 Manor Place
Edinburgh EH3 7DD
Tel: 0131 226 6051
Fax: 0131 225 9833
www.scottisharts.org.uk

Scottish Civic Trust (The)
The Tobacco Merchant's House
42 Miller Street
Glasgow G1 1DT
Tel: 0141 221 1466
Fax: 0141 248 6952
www.scottishcivictrust.org.uk

Scottish Convention Bureau
23 Ravelston Terrace
Edinburgh EH4 3EU
Tel: 0131 343 1608
Fax: 0131 343 1844
www.conventionscotland.com

Sport Scotland
Caledonia House
South Gyle
Edinburgh EH12 9DQ
Tel: 0131 317 7200
Fax: 0131 317 7202

Scottish Tourist Board (The)
23 Ravelston Terrace
Edinburgh EH4 3EU
Tel: 0131 332 2433
Fax: 0131 313 1513
www.visitscotland.com

Sport England
16 Upper Woburn Place
London WC1H 0QP
Tel: 020 7273 1500
Fax: 020 7383 5740
www.sportengland.org

Sports Council for Wales (The)
Sophia Gardens
Cardiff CF1 9SW
Tel: 029 2030 0500
Fax: 029 2030 0600
www.sports-council-wales.co.uk

Sports Sponsorship Advisory Service
Francis House
Francis Street, London SW1P 1DE
Tel: 020 7854 8598
Fax: 020 7854 8501
www.sponsorship-advice.org

Skills Active (formerly SPRITO)
24 Stephenson Way
London NW1 2HD
Tel: 020 7388 7755
Fax: 020 7388 9733
www.sprito.org.uk

Stagesafe
13 Portland Road
Street
Somerset BA16 9PX
Tel: 01458 445186
Fax: 01458 841186
www.stagesafe.co.uk

Tourism Society
1-2 Queen Victoria Terrace
Sovereign Court
London E1W 3HA
Tel: 020 7488 2789
Fax: 020 7488 9148
www.tourismsociety.org

Two Four Productions Limited
Quay West Studios
Old Newnham
Plymouth PL7 5BH
Tel: 01752 333900
Fax: 01752 344224
www.twofour.co.uk

UK:Athletics
10 Athletics House
Harbourne Road
Edgbaston
Birmingham B15 3AA
Tel: 0121 456 5098
Fax: 0121 456 8752
www.ukathletics.net

UK Sport
40 Bernard Street
London WC1N 1ST
Tel: 020 7211 5100
Fax: 020 7211 5246
www.uksport.gov.uk

Wales Tourist Board (The)
Brunel House
2 Fitzgalan Street
Cardiff CF24 0UY
Tel: 029 2049 9909
Fax: 029 2048 5031
www.wtbonline.gov.uk

Weather Direct
One America Square
17 Crosswall
London EC3N 2LB
Tel: 020 7426 4651
Fax: 020 7680 4080
www.weatherdirect.co.uk

Welsh Arts Council (The)
9 Museum Place
Cardiff F10 3NX
Tel: 029 2037 6500
Fax: 029 2022 1447
www.artswales.org

West Berkshire Council
Council Offices
Market Place
Newbury
Berkshire RG14 5LD
Tel: 01635 424000
Fax: 01635 519431
www.westberks.gov.uk

Zap Productions Ltd
3rd Floor, 7A Middle Street
Brighton
East Sussex BN1 1AL
Tel: 01273 821588
Fax: 01273 206960
www.zapproductions.co.uk

b) reading list

Bibliography

BOOKS

These books are available from ILAM. The ILAM Bookshop can also supply a complete list of leisure related titles. Please contact the Bookshop for further information on tel: 01491 874842

ALLEN, J., ET. AL., *Festival and special event management,* WILEY 2002
An introduction to the principles of planning, managing and staging festivals and special events. Includes guidance on logistics, marketing and promotion, and evaluation. 416pp

ALLEN, J., *The business of event planning,* WILEY 2002
Practical tools and expert advice for professional event planners. Explains every aspect of organising and strategic planning for events which includes preparing proposals, setting fees, designing multicultural events and using efficient new technologies. 329pp

ALLEN, J. *Event planning,* WILEY 2000
Takes you through every aspect of organising and executing a successful event.

AMERICAN SPORT EDUCATION PROGRAM,
Event management for sports directors, HUMAN KINETICS 1996
Designed as a tool for the planning and managing any type or size of athletic event. Areas covered include: event objectives; finances; rules and officials; coach development; risk management; registration; practice and competition schedules; facility needs; equipment, uniforms and supplies; awards; food service; transportation; housing; promotion; public relations; communications; event evaluation; staffing. 131pp

BADMIN, P.; COOMBS, M.; RAYNER, G.,
Leisure operational management. Vol 1 : Facilities. (Longman/ILAM Leisure Management Series), LONGMAN 1988
A student textbook and reference book for practising facility managers covering the following topics: programming, multi-use and joint provision, sponsorship and special event organisation. 159pp., illus., tables, refs.

BATES., WELLS, BRAITHWAITE, *Fundraisers guide to the law,* DIRECTORY OF SOCIAL CHANGE, 2000
A guide for fundraisers to the laws that effect fundraising for charities. Information is supplemented by detailed list of useful addresses, a series of sample legal contracts and comprehensive index.

BOTTING, N.; NORTON, M., *Complete fundraising handbook, 4th edition,* DIRECTORY OF SOCIAL CHANGE, 2001
Offers down to earth advice on every aspect of raising money for charity. 356pp

BOWDIN, GLENN; ET AL, *Events management,* BUTTERWORTH HEINEMANN 2001
A guide to the processes of events management from creation and planning to staging and evaluation. Includes examples of key concepts within case studies. Intended for academic students and those taking management development training. 321pp

CARNIE, C., *Find the funds,* DIRECTORY OF SOCIAL CHANGE, 2000
Includes sources lists with details of more than 120 publications, websites and agencies, an appendix of photocopiable charts for planning research and recording data.

EASTWOOD, N., MOUNTFIELD, A., *Funding guide: Schools,* DIRECTORY OF SOCIAL CHANGE, 2001
Lists over 200 potential sources of funding for primary and secondary schools.

EASTWOOD, N., *Youth funding guide, 2nd edition,* DIRECTORY OF SOCIAL CHANGE, 2002
Offers practical advice on fundraising for youth related causes. Includes: budgeting, fundraising, writing applications, raising money. Also details sources of funding, National Lottery, grant making Trusts, companies, national and regional local government, and the European Union.

FORRESTER, SUSAN; LLOYD, DAVID, *Arts funding guide,* DIRECTORY OF SOCIAL CHANGE 2002
UK sources of funding for all art forms, arts organisations and arts events. Covers financial and enterprise/management support from government sources, Europe, trusts and companies. Funder profiles give information on policy and funding criteria to help you target your applications successfully. 560pp

FROSDICK, S.; WALLEY, L., *Sport and safety management,* BUTTERWORTH HEINEMANN 1999
A comprehensive and practical handbook for all involved with the safe management at sporting events. Brings together research, best practice and advice for managing the safety of all sports stadia. Paperback

GOLDBLATT, J.J., *Special events: Twenty-first century global event management,* WILEY 2002
A special events reference work examining and explaining event administration, coordination, marketing and management, and looking at legal, ethical and risk management in relation to events. Also examines modern events technology, and career advancement within events work. Appendices include a range of sample agreements, orders, reports and menus. 459pp

GOLDBLATT, J; NELSON, K S, *International dictionary of event management,* JOHN WILEY & SONS 2001
New edition of the comprehensive guide to the vocabulary of event management - with almost 4,000 terms covered. 279pp

GOLDBLATT, J., *Dollars and events: how to succeed in the special events business,* WILEY 1999
Written specifically for aspiring and established special events professionals, this provides all the information needed to start, grow and manage special events - related business or career. Learn how to develop a vision, mission, and a strategy, manage finances, find the capital, create a marketing plan, hire and keep employees to help business thrive. 298pp

GOLDBLATT, J., *Special events: best practice in modern event management,* VAN NOSTRAND REINHOLD 1997
A comprehensive study of the special events field including case studies. Covers scheduling, organisation, marketing.

GRAY, J.; ELSDEN, S. *Organising special events for fundraising and campaigning*, 2000
Illustrated by case studies from the British Red Cross this includes setting objectives, finding innovative ideas, planning and budgeting, choosing venues and recruiting patrons, dealing with the public and talking to the media.

HEALTH AND SAFETY EXECUTIVE, *Event safety guide: a guide to health, safety and welfare at music and similar events*, HSE BOOKS 1999
Guidance covering crowd management, safety, stewarding, facilities for people with disabilities, barriers, marquees and large tents, special effects, lighting and electrical installations, sound and noise and waste disposal. Replaces 1993 edition published as Guide to health, safety and welfare at pop concerts and similar events. 218pp

HOYLE, L.H., *Event marketing: How to successfully promote events, festivals, conventions, and expositions*, WILEY, 2002
Provides the tools required to carry out every phase of a successful, integrated marketing campaign for any event, from conferences and expositions to fairs and festivals that host 20,000 people. Includes: overview of event promotion, advertising, public relations, electronic marketing strategies, and budget funding. In depth analysis of marketing for specific events, examination of future trends, innovative strategies for increasing attendance with comprehensive appendices are also included. 224pp

INSIDE COMMUNICATIONS, *The White Book 2003 edition*, INSIDE COMMUNICATIONS, 2003
A comprehensive international directory listing suppliers to the arts, entertainment and media industries. Including lists of agents, artists, services and equipment for the film, television and conference industries, UK venues and other professional services.

JOBBER, D., *Principles and practice of marketing, 3rd edition*, MCGRAW-HILL, 2000
Offers a clear explanation of the theory of marketing practice taking into account today's greater emphasis on direct marketing and relationship marketing.

KYAMBALESA, H., *Marketing in the 21st Century: Concepts, Challenges and Imperative*, ASHGATE, 2000
Designed to explore emerging challenges for marketers, as well as to survey viable strategies for meeting these challenges. A 'how-to' book for both prospective and practising marketers. Updates many traditional marketing concepts and terminologies now considered unsuitable due to innovations in business practices and modes of operations dictated by change in social, economic, competitive and technological conditions.

McCABE, V.; POOLE, B., ET AL, *Business and Management of Conventions*, WILEY 2000
A text introducing the meetings, incentives, conventions and exhibitions (MICE) industry. Looks at the worldwide market and specifically Australia where the market has increased substantially and which is considered to be a major player.

McDONNELL, I.; ALLEN, J., *Festival and special event management*, WILEY 1999
An introduction to the principles associated with planning, managing and staging festivals and special events. A textbook for students studying event management containing case studies. Australian publication.

McDONALD, M., *Marketing Plans: How to prepare them, how to use them, 5th edition*, BUTTERWORTH HEINEMANN, 2002
This new edition, thoroughly revised and updated throughout, provides a practical, hands-on approach for implementing every single concept included in the text. Features include: key concepts, crucial terms, examples, headlines, marketing insights, case studies and exercises. Recommended for professional marketers and students of marketing, both undergraduates and those on professional courses or CIM and CAM.

MELDRUM, M.; McDONALD, M, *Marketing in manageable bites for busy managers and overworked students*, 2000
Offers concise, stand-alone, summaries of marketing principles, concepts, tools and techniques. Covers over 50 fundamental marketing topics, each presented as a discrete discussion of the key issues involved.

O'TOOLE, W; MIKOLAITIS, P., *Corporate event project management*, WILEY 2002
This book merges event and project management to provide a new set of tools to guide the user through every aspect of planning and managing a corporate event. 285pp

ROGERS, T., *Conferences: a 21st century industry*, ADDISON WESLEY LONGMAN 1998
Analyses the conference and meeting industry detailing its structure and trends and assessing its size and economic value. Traces the evolution of the industry, identifies key players and covers the principles and practice of successful conference and event management.

SHONE, A., *The business of conferences*, BUTTERWORTH HEINEMANN 1998
Considers the nature and background of the UK and Irish conference industries and looks at the management issues involved in professional and competitive conferencing.

SKINNER, B.E.; RUKAVINA, V., *Event Sponsorship*, WILEY 2003
Provides step-by-step guidelines for attracting, signing and keeping sponsorship for any event, including festivals, conventions, expositions, sporting events, arts and entertainment spectaculars, charity benefits and much more. Presents successful strategies and tools for staying competitive in today's market.

SMYTH, J., *Guide to UK Company giving 2002, 4th edition*, DIRECTORY OF SOCIAL CHANGE, 2002
Fully updated to include details of over 550 companies in the UK that give a combined total of £450 million in community support - including £280 million in cash donations to voluntary and community organisations. Entries include: contact details, examples of grants, typical grant ranges, and advice.

STAYTE, S., *Conference organiser's timesaver*, ILAM, 2002
Provides prepared forms, schedules and checklists which can be adapted to suit individual organisations' needs. Compiled to complement individuals own planning activities to make the job of conference organiser easier. Forms are also included on an enclosed CD in Microsoft format. 68pp

TARLOW, P.E., *Event risk management and safety*, JOHN WILEY AND SONS 2002
This book provides assistance to event organisers, managers, and planners to reduce, in some cases eliminate the thousands of accidents arising in injury, death and financial loss that can and do occur at events each year. 272pp

TORKILDSEN, G., *Leisure and recreation management*, E & F N SPON 1999
Textbook covering key concepts, trends, provision, management and operation of leisure management. This fourth edition undergraduate textbook contains four parts: leisure and the needs of the people; leisure trends, planning and the government; the leisure providers; the management of leisure.

VEN DEN BERG, L; BRAUN, E; OTGAAR, A.H.J., *Sports and city marketing in European cities*, ASHGATE 2002
Sports events may also help to promote the city where such events take place, and urban management policies are increasingly taking advantage of sports events or clubs to promote the location, and maximize potential revenue. A look at city marketing policies in five cities - Helsinki, Rotterdam, Barcelona, Manchester and Turin. 125pp

WATT, D., *Event management in leisure and tourism*, ADDISON WESLEY LONGMAN 1998
Provides a comprehensive overview of event management and organisation for events industry practitioners and students. Real life examples are used to enhance understanding of theory and case studies of major projects in action are featured. Includes revision questions for students on degree and HND/C courses.

WATT, D., *Sports management and administration*, ROUTLEDGE, 2003
This text is designed to help all those delivering sport to deliver it better and includes: the voluntary sector; event management and marketing; marketing, fundraising and sponsorship; managing staff and volunteers; organisational management principles; legal issues including health and safety; and case studies - both local and national. 280pp

WELLS, C., *Finding Company Sponsors for Good Causes*, DIRECTORY OF SOCIAL CHANGE, 2000
This book will help fundraisers secure company sponsorship and advises on how to approach the potential sponsor, target the proposal, set a sponsorship fee and negotiate a deal and manage the project.

ILAM 101 Ways Series

BONE, V.; MITCHELL, B., *101 Ways to Succeed in Developing Cultural Strategies*, ILAM 2000
Based on the authors' experiences in producing cultural strategies, it also draws upon work carried out in a range of local authorities, pilots, and non pilots, to illustrate key points within a series of case studies. It is intended to be read as complementary to both the DCMS Guidance and the CLOA Good Practice Guide.

ILAM BEST VALUE WORKING GROUP, *101 Ways to approach a best value review*, ILAM 2000
From the initial scoping of a review, through to inspection, every aspect of implementing best value reviews is easily explained. It offers a logical step by step approach to the four C's and in addition fully covers all other key aspects.

GOODING, A., *101 Ways to succeed in sports development, 3rd edition*, ILAM 2003
Topics covered include equal opportunities, marketing, sponsorship, developing partnerships, performance measurement and working with volunteers.

ELLISON, E., *101 Ways to implement the disability discrimination act (DDA)*, ILAM 2001
Step by step guidance on all aspects of the Disability Discrimination Act. Highlights the areas and actions that organisations and managers need to be aware of and to take action with, to comply with the requirements of access and equality exemplified by the Act.

WALTON, M., *101 Ways to manage a children's activity programme*, ILAM 2001
This publication has been written with the aim of providing effective and functional guidelines for best practice within an activity setting. Aimed at leisure and community service providers, schools, individuals and those responsible for the provision for children outside school hours.

The books listed here can be viewed at ILAM's Information Centre. In addition to this, the Information Centre can provide reading lists on event related topics from its database containing reference books, reports and journal articles. Please contact the ILAM Information Centre for further details on tel: 01491 874841 or email: infocentre@ilam.co.uk